THE
POSTCOLONIAL
BIBLE

edited by

R.S. Sugirtharajah

THE BIBLE AND POSTCOLONIALISM, 1

Series Editor:

R.S. Sugirtharajah

Sheffield
Academic Press

Published by
Sheffield Academic Press Ltd
Mansion House
19 Kingfield Road
Sheffield S11 9AS
England

Typeset by Sheffield Academic Press
and
Printed on acid-free paper in Great Britain
by Biddles Ltd
King's Lynn, Norfolk

British Library Cataloguing in Publication Data

A catalogue record for this book is available
from the British Library

ISBN 1-85075-898-0

Contents

Part I
Introduction

Part II
Discursive Spaces

Acknowledgments

In preparing this volume, I have been supported and helped by a number of people. My deep appreciation goes to Sheffield Academic Press, especially their directors—David Clines, Philip Davies and Jean Allen—for agreeing to launch a series on the Bible and Postcolonialism, and their confidence in the project, and especially to Jean for all her encouragement and patience; Rebecca Cullen for shepherding this volume through the editorial process with efficency and care; Webb Mealy for his perceptive part in initiating the project; Ralph Broadbent for his technical expertise in sorting out the arcane world of computer programmes and his help in preparing the text for the Press; the contributors to this volume for their enthusiastic support of the project; Dr Dan O'Connor for his continued friendship and inspiration; the Pollock Memorial Missionary Trust for a grant towards editorial and secretarial expenses; Selly Oak Colleges Central Library staff—Meline Nielson, Sue Abbott, Michael Gale, Ben Taylor and Griselda Lartey—for their willingness to go an extra mile to help with my enquiries; and finally, my wife Sharada for her keen interest and support for all that I do.

R.S. Sugirtharajah
Selly Oak Colleges
Birmingham

List of Contributors

ROLAND BOER
United Theological College, North Parrammatta, NSW, Australia

RANDALL C. BAILEY
Interdenominational Theological Centre, Atlanta, GA, USA

MUSA W. DUBE
University of Botswana, Gaborone, Botswana

RICHARD A. HORSLEY
University of Massachusetts, Boston, USA

KWOK PUI-LAN
Episcopal Divinity School, Cambridge, MA, USA

SHARON H. RINGE
Wesley Theological Seminary, Washington, USA

FERNANDO F. SEGOVIA
Vanderbilt University, Nashville, TN, USA

R.S. SUGIRTHARAJAH
Selly Oak Colleges, Birmingham, England

BASTIAAN WIELENGA
Tamilnadu Theological Seminary, Madurai, South India

Abbreviations

AB	Anchor Bible
ATR	*Anglican Theological Review*
BibInt	*Biblical Interpretation: A Journal of Contemporary Approaches*
CBQ	*Catholic Biblical Quarterly*
HTR	*Harvard Theological Review*
Int	*Interpretation*
JAAR	*Journal of the American Academy of Religion*
JBL	*Journal of Biblical Literature*
JITC	*Journal of the Interdenomination Theological Center*
JSNT	*Journal for the Study of the New Testament*
NICNT	New International Commentary on the New Testament
PSB	*Princeton Seminary Bulletin*
PTCA	*Programme for Theology and Cultures in Asia Bulletin*
ZRGG	*Zeitschrift für Religions- und Geistesgeschichte*

PART I

INTRODUCTION

Biblical Studies after the Empire: From A Colonial to a Postcolonial Mode of Interpretation

R.S. SUGIRTHARAJAH

I start not with Christian texts but with colonial cartoons.

The first is a lithograph, 'James Rennell's Map of Hindoostan' (1782) (Fig. 1), Rennell being the Surveyor-General of Bengal at that time, and known as 'the father of Indian geography'. It is a crowded picture, full of people, tools, texts and a temple tower. There are Indians, probably Brahmins, British civilians and Britannia; on the ground are tools such as are used by map-makers and surveyors and in the background is the temple tower. We also note that texts are being exchanged, one of which has *Shaster* written on it. Crucial to the picture is this exchange of texts. At a first glance, it may appear that Britannia, standing upright and fully clothed, with the temple tower behind her, like a Queen/ goddess, is trying to deliver *Shaster* to complaisant and half-naked Indians. But a closer look will reveal that it is Britannia who is receiving the document from the Indian, with other Indians waiting to make their offerings—no doubt in exchange for Rennell's map. They appear to be entrusting *Shaster*, India's cultural treasury, her learning, religious and legal wisdom, to Britannia. The gesture is significant for Britain's transformation from being a trading company to ruler of India's territories. It also gives out another signal: it is the end of the British reliance on local interpreters. From now on the British will translate, interpret and reign without the intervention of the natives. In this inversion of roles, it is the British who will in future hand back *shastras* to the Indians, who will depend on the British for the proper interpretation of their own literary, legal and sacred texts. Thus Britain

Fig. 1. Lithograph, 'James Rennell's Map of Hindoostan.' From his *Memoir of a Map of Hindoostan, or the Moghul's Empire.*

assumes the mantle of patron, provider, supplier and superinten-
dent of authentic information and exposition about all things
related to India and the Orient.

The second (Fig. 2) is an oil painting by Jones Barker. This
time, an African, perhaps a prince, is being presented with the
Bible by Queen Victoria in the audience chamber at Windsor in
1861. Queen Victoria, in the presence of Prince Albert, Viscount
Palmerston and Lord John Russell, is gifting to the African,
England's greatest cultural product, the English Bible, possibly
the King James Version, a book in which 'not a single line was
written, or single thought was conceived by, an Englishman'
(Baikie 1928: 7). A collection of books which originated in West
Asia, rooted in Mediterranean cultural values, clothed in the
everyday imagery of Semitic and Hellenistic peoples, has now
been assimilated by the English, reinscribed into their linguistic,
poetic forms, and turned into a cultural artefact of the English
people. From now on, it will be distributed throughout the world

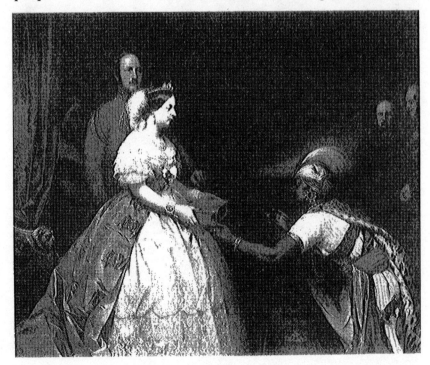

Fig. 2. Queen Victoria presenting a Bible in the Audience Chamber at
Windsor, by T. Jones Barker c. 1861.

as an icon containing civilizing properties. The African, kneeling, represents the heathen foreigner whose moral improvement was seen as the responsibility of the English.

Let us leave aside for a moment these colonial cartoons and turn our attention to the current state of biblical scholarship. Anyone who is familiar with writing on recent trends will know that it has been going through different phases, often described as precritical, critical and postcritical, sometimes as historical and narrative, or author-centred, text-centred and reader-centred. These phases describe how it has been seen from a Western perspective. Those of us who have been at the receiving end of colonialism would want to present biblical scholarship as falling into two categories—colonial and postcolonial.

Colonial reading can be summed up as informed by theories concerning the innate superiority of Western culture, the Western male as subject, and the natives, heathens, women, blacks, indigenous people, as the Other, needing to be controlled and subjugated. It is based on the desire for power/domination. Swami Vivekananda, the Indian saint, was not far from the truth when he thundered at the first Parliament of Religions at Chicago: 'You come with the Bible in one hand and the conqueror's sword in the other.'[1] Colonial intentions were reinforced by the replacement of indigenous reading practices, negative representations of the 'natives', and the employment of exegetical strategies in the commentarial writings and hermeneutical discourses that legitimized imperial control.[2]

The current move towards a postcolonial biblical criticism, seeks to overturn colonial assumptions. The term 'postcolonial' itself is a complex one and has been much contested.[3] The

1. See *The Missionary Review of the World* 17 (12), 1894, p. 882.
2. See Sugirtharajah 1996, for Joachim Jeremias's negative representations of the people of the East. For how exegesis was used to legitimize colonial rule see Sugirtharajah, forthcoming.
3. The literature on postcolonialism is massive, and continually keeps growing. For a discussion of the term, and explication of postcolonial modes of theorizing, see Ashcroft, Griffiths and Tiffin (1989, 1995); Williams and Chrisman (1993); Mongia (1996); Chambers and Curti (1996); Moore-Gilbert (1997); Childs and Williams (1997). For a searching and healthily sceptical critique, see Ahmad (1992); Shohat (1992); McClintock (1992); Miyoshi (1993); Dirlik (1994); Trivedi and Mukherjee (1996).

situation is further complicated by the different forms and histories of colonialism, accompanied by processes of decolonization
which have been equally varied and complex. The major achieve-
ment of postcolonialism is to inaugurate a new era of academic
inquiry which brings to the fore the overlapping issues of empire,
nation, ethnicity, migration and language. Where it differs from
earlier critical theories is that the postcolonial discourse impli-
cates academic learning in colonialism. It challenges the context,
contours and normal procedures of biblical scholarship. In this
volume, postcolonialism is roughly defined as scrutinizing and
exposing colonial domination and power as these are embodied
in biblical texts and in interpretations, and as searching for alternative hermeneutics while thus overturning and dismantling colonial perspectives. What postcolonialism does is to enable us to
question the totalizing tendencies of European reading practices
and interpret the texts on our own terms and read them from our
specific locations.

Earlier Incursions

Examining the text for its colonial connotations or interrogating
the interpretation for its colonial intentions is not totally new.
There have been a few preliminary attempts in the past that
addressed postcolonial concerns without using the current theoretical categories. Roy Sano, an Asian-American writing in the
1970s, castigated the neo-orthodox theology of the time, and the
failure of the heirs of Niebuhr to recognize the 'category of the
empire for Christian thought and action':

> They talked about particular evils, and even if they spoke of institu-
> tional or systemic evils, they failed to employ the category of
> empire as an organizing principle, much less locate the seat of the
> empire in their own country (1979: 257).

Roy Sano also took up the issues of the immigration history and
memory of Asian-Americans and addressed the hermeneutical
implications of a community living in diaspora. He endeavoured
to work out a hermeneutics that made better sense of the experience and status of immigrants in America. Constantly faced with
negative portrayals of American immigrant communities, Sano
turned to biblical narratives to celebrate and reinforce their

ethnicity and to affirm their status of rootlessness. Rejecting the assimilative narrative position advocated by the book of Ruth, he opted for Esther as the appropriate model, for she not only succeeded in an alien world concealing her Jewishness, but, once she was established, recovered her identity, and, at the risk of her own life, was able to overturn the decree that went against her people. Sano also found the apocalyptic writers more useful than the prophets. The penchant for prophetic writing among white theologians, he alleged, was due to the fact that both operate in an established nation-state, and have access to power. The apocalyptic literature, on the other hand, is suited to immigrants, because this genre emerged at a time in Israel's history when she had lost her sovereignty. More importantly, the apocalyptic writings envisage a total social and political discontinuity and a reversal of roles rather than piecemeal changes. Despite the historical and theological defects of apocalypticism, Sano reckoned that it gave Asian-Americans a renewed consciousness.

Similarly in the 1980s, the Indian theologian Samuel Rayan explored the hermeneutical implications of the political, cultural and economic imperialism exerted by the USA, Russia, Europe and Japan. He turned to Jesus and Roman-occupied, first-century Palestine. Rayan conceded that Jesus did not clash openly with the Roman authorities, but he directed his anger towards Israel's internal imperialism and the collaborators of the Roman Empire: 'He understood imperialism when he refused to submit or conform to the powers that be...' (1985b: 106). In his study of the tribute-money incident, Rayan shows how, at the height of modern colonialism, biblical interpreters tended to take an 'anti-Zealot and pro-Roman' stance and later, during the period of decolonization after the Second World War, questioned such a reading, and advocated an 'anti-imperialist stance and the affirmation of freedom' (p. 90).

In addressing colonial issues, Sano and Rayan worked within the currently available framework of Christian categories, which were shaped by the demands and pressures of liberation theology which was making a forceful entry at that time. They utilized and rehabilitated Christian concepts as a way out of the colonial mess. While Sano advocated the liberation of the ethnic communities in preference to the reconciliation advocated by the neo-orthodoxy

of the time, Rayan emphasized the Christian faith as a revolutionary force which carried within it the power to combat all structures which exploit, enslave and dehumanize people.

In the subsequent emergence of dalit, feminist, tribal and
Burakumin theologies, with their existential concern for emancipation from the stigma attached to caste, gender and community,
the legacy of colonialism and a whole variety of texts and practices
that were associated with it went unnoticed and unacknowledged
in Asian hermeneutics. In other words, in the subalterns' under-
standable urgency to recover their self-identity, the matters of
colony and empire, although they had been instrumental in
marginalizing these sectors, were pushed aside and accorded
secondary importance.

However, the emergence in the field of humanities of systematic scrutiny of the historical records of colonialism in the field of
humanities and of the changes that the imperial experience has
produced in identity, practice, knowledge, and the hermeneutical
connection between interpretation, mission and colonial expansion, has provided a compelling reason for biblical scholarship to
re-examine the interrelatedness of interpretation and colonialism.

About This Volume

What this collection of essays is trying to do is to follow the
Saidian exhortation to peruse the texts for the gaps, absences and
ellipses, the silences and closures, and so facilitate the recovery of
history or narrative that has been suppressed or distorted. The
chapters that comprise this volume emanate from various social
locations and are naturally varied, but are tacitly connected. They
all speak to the shared concern with colonialism, territorial or
discursive, or both, and how colonialism reinscribes itself, sometimes discretely, at times overtly, in biblical discourse and how it
may be dismantled.

The essays appear in four sections, but these divisions have
more to do with a conventional table of contents, and as readers
will note, the essays transgress these boundaries. Moreover, the
categorization is somewhat arbitrary and does not do justice to the
cross- and multi-disciplinary interventions and investments of the
essayists.

The second section opens with an essay by Roland Boer. In it he sets himself three tasks—to theorize postcolonialism; to investigate (post) colonial biblical studies in Australia, and to set goals for future non-hegemonic reading practice. His characterization of Australian biblical scholarship in terms of the clichés of colonial existence—tyranny of distance, cultural hierarchy and cultural cringe, with its characteristics of 'emulation', 'nationalistic' and 'positively unoriginal'—could well have been said about other countries which have come under the heavy influence of colonialism. In the final part of the essay, investigating the possibilities for postcolonial biblical studies in and from Australia, Boer suggests that the subversion of hegemonic biblical criticism is yoked to the socialist promise of postcolonialism by tying it in with Marxist literary theory and criticism. Fernando Segovia, in placing postcolonial biblical interpretation within the critical paradigm of cultural studies, deals with the relationship between the proposed biblical hermeneutics and postcolonial theory and discourse. He identifies three postcolonial optics—the shadows of empire in the production of texts of Judaism and early Christianity; the colonial imperatives that surround Western interpretations of Jewish and Christian texts, and the emergence of biblical critics from the former empire who are trying to subvert the received readings. The hermeneutical goal for Segovia is not only analysis and description, but transformation. Randall Bailey explores and critiques the various modes of Afrocentric biblical interpretation undertaken by the African diasporan community and how they have functioned throughout their history. My essay, while celebrating the inauguration of postcolonial theory, also points out its shortcomings. The main part of my essay is spent in examining the interrelatedness of mission, interpretation and colonialism. I take another look at two biblical texts, Mt. 28.19 and the Pauline missionary tours, and demonstrate how the reactivation of these texts during the territorial expansion of European nations provided scriptural sanction for and legitimized colonial enterprises.

In the third section, Dube, reading the Johannine gospel in conjunction with two other texts, the *Aeneid* and the *Heart of Darkness*, contends that the Johannine approach of exalting Jesus to divine status above all Jewish and other religious figures of the world, is not so different from the colonial ideology embedded in the characterization of colonizing agents—Kurtz and Aeneas. Dube's plea is to strip off the colonial ideology of the Johannine text and work out a hermeneutics that would lay emphasis on a liberating interdependence between colonizer and colonized, male–female, North–South. Sharon Ringe speaks to the ambivalent situation of feminists in a hegemonic culture like the USA, where the feminists find themselves both colonizers and colonized. As women, she points out, they have been weighed down under the political and discursive colonial project of kyriarchy. As members of the dominant culture, they cannot fight their own colonial status without also participating in systems that express and support various colonial projects of Euro-American capitalism. In her essay, Ringe explores this historical ambivalence and its impact on biblical interpretation through the lens of the teachings on table community in Lk. 14.1, 7-14. Her study investigates values, presuppositions and social codes embedded in the Lukan narrative and the intersection with women, both ancient and current readers. The issues of postcoloniality are not confined to centres outside Europe. Richard Horsley, after offering a critical prolegomenon to the project of postcolonial criticism, goes on to explore the previously submerged (colonized) histories of the Jesus movement and the Pauline communities which became victims of the grand narratives of Western Christianity. He rescues Mark and Paul from the essentialist, individualist and depoliticized Western readings, and reconfigures how Mark and Paul explore some of the ways that not only resist the dominant imperial culture in their writings but proceed with building or restoration of communities alternative to the imperial order in the movements they represent.

The essays in the final section employ a variety of strategies. Adopting the rhetoric of dialogue, and mobilizing the insights gleaned from postcolonial criticism, Kwok Pui-lan investigates the social and cultural web undergirding the latest quest for Jesus. The first quest for the historical Jesus coincided with Europe's imperative of discovering distant lands and civilizing the natives, while the latest quest is taking place at a time when white male power has been decentralizeded and when the natives are exerting power in the land of hope and glory. The final essay is an example in autobiographical criticism. In a reflective mood, Bas

Wielenga situates the Jacob–Esau story in several different colonial sites varying from Dutch territorial colonialism to the enthnonationalism of Sri Lanka. Wielenga shows that the Jacob–Esau story, rather than being a repository of fixed meanings, is open to multiple interpretations, and takes on a hermeneutical life of its own in different colonial and neocolonial locations where the meanings are produced and reproduced to suit the occasion. What is significant in his essay is that he goes beyond the personal narration and teases out the implications of the text at a time when greed and accumulation, orchestrated by global capitalism, are seen as normal and normative behaviour. The challenge that Wielenga poses is whether, like Esau, we can say, 'It is enough. Let me share.'

Now to return to the cartoons. What we see in them is the depiction of subject people as passive and docile, as the colonialists imagined and wanted to depict them. What postcolonialism does is to reverse this depiction and overturn the stereotypical images of colonialism and assert the authenticity of the 'natives' as subjects and their desire to be independent and, when necessary, troublesome and seditious. Postcoloniality does not mean happiness and prosperity for all. What is certain is that postcolonialism will continue to challenge the context and contours of biblical interpretation, and the existing notions and preconceptions of professional guilds and academies. If this volume can make a minor stir in the normal procedures of scholarly circles and chip away at their foundations a bit, the essayists will be more than pleased.

BIBLIOGRAPHY

Ahmad, Aijaz
    1992   *In Theory: Classes, Nations, Literatures* (London: Verso).
Ashcroft, Bill, Gareth Griffiths and Helen Tiffin (eds.)
    1989   *The Empire Writes Back: Theory and Practice in Post-Colonial Literatures* (London: Routledge & Kegan Paul).
    1995   *The Post-Colonial Studies Reader* (London: Routledge & Kegan Paul).
Baikie, James
    1928   *The English Bible and its Story: Its Growth, its Translators and their Adventures* (London: Seeley, Service).
Chambers, Iain, and Lidia Curti (eds.)
    1996   *The Post-Colonial Question: Common Skies, Divided Horizons* (London: Routledge & Kegan Paul).

Childs, Peter, and Patrick R.J. Williams
    1997   *An Introduction to Post-Colonial Theory* (London: Prentice–Hall).
Dirlik, Arif
    1994   'The Postcolonial Aura: Third World Criticism in the Age of Global
                Capitalism', *Critical Inquiry* 20 (2): 328-56; reprinted in Mongia
                1996: 294-320.
McClintock, Anne
    1992   'The Angel of Progress: Pitfalls of the term "Post-colonialism"',
                Social Text 31 (32): 84-98; reprinted in Williams and Chrisman 1993:
                291-304.
The Missionary Review of the World
    1894   'The Parliament of Religions: A Review' 17 (12): 881-94.
Miyoshi, Masao
    1993   'A Borderless World?: From Colonialism to Transnationalism and
                the Decline of the Nation-State', *Critical Inquiry* 19: 726-51.
Mongia, Padmini
    1996   *Contemporary Postcolonial Theory: A Reader* (London: Arnold).
Moore-Gilbert, Bart
    1997   *Postcolonial Theory: Contexts, Practices, Politics* (London: Verso).
Rayan, S.
    1985a   'Caesar Versus God', in S. Kappen (ed.), *Jesus Today* (Bombay:
                AICUF Publication): 88-97.
    1985b   'Jesus and Imperialism', in S. Kappen (ed.), *Jesus Today* (Bombay:
                AICUF Publication): 98-117.
Sano, Roy I.
    1979   'Ethnic Liberation Theology: Neo-Orthodoxy Reshaped or
                Replaced', in Gerald H. Anderson and Thomas F. Stransky (eds.),
                Mission Trends 4: Liberation Theologies (New York: Paulist Press): 247-
                58. The original piece appeared in *Christianity and Crisis: A Christian
                Journal of Opinion* 35 (1975): 258-64.
Shohat, Ella
    1992   'Notes on the "Post-Colonial"', *Social Text* 31 (32): 99-113; reprinted
                in Mongia 1996: 321-34.
Sugirtharajah, R.S.
    1996   'Orientalism, Ethnonationalism and Transnationalism: Shifting
                Identities and Biblical Interpretation', in Mark G. Brett (ed.), *Eth-
                nicity and the Bible* (Leiden: E.J. Brill).
 Forthcoming   'Imperial Critical Commentaries: Christian Discourse and Com-
                mentarial Writings in Colonial India', in *idem* (ed.), *Asian Biblical
                Hermeneutics and Postcolonialism: Contesting the Interpretations* (Mary-
                knoll, NY: Orbis Books).
Trivedi, Harish, and Meenakshi Mukherjee (eds.)
    1996   *Interrogating Post-Colonialism: Theory, Practice and Context* (Shimla:
                Indian Institute of Advanced Study).
Williams, Patrick, and Laura Chrisman (eds.)
    1993   *Colonial Discourse and Post-colonial Theory: A Reader* (Hemel Hemp-
                stead: Harvester Wheatsheaf).

PART II

DISCURSIVE SPACES

Remembering Babylon:
Postcolonialism and Australian Biblical Studies

ROLAND BOER

Postcolonialism, understood for the moment as a heterogeneous discourse, is not something that is particularly well known in the circle of biblical studies in Australia, a situation that indicates a great deal about biblical studies in this formerly colonial nation-state. And yet the paradox here is that both colonialism and post-colonialism, now understood in terms of overlapping periods of socio-economic and cultural history, have been and remain formative influences on the way biblical studies is practised in Australia. In introducing the issues in such a way I have already indicated the topics that are important for this essay: how one might speak of postcolonialism, particularly in the context of Australia, and the practice of biblical studies in the same place. Yet it is the contradiction inherent in the relationship between these two topics that interests me, namely, the importance of postcolonialism for Australian biblical studies and the lack of awareness of that significance, a lack of consciousness—perhaps even an unconscious—which in turn makes postcolonialism even more potent.

In broaching this topic I am allowing the theoretical to take flight in a situation where this causes me some unease, since my gut instinct is to prefer textual analysis over against theoretical elaboration. The theoretical has its own place, however, particularly when there is a need to reflect on the nature of postcolonialism as such, given the too-rapid assumption in many cases that the meaning of 'postcolonialism' itself is reasonably secure. After postcolonialism itself, I will turn to consider the nature of biblical studies in (post)colonial Australia, something I intend not to be a

survey so much as an attempt to track down some of the contradictions that have and continue to characterize this particular
academic and confessional discipline. This is facilitated by considering some clichés of popular (academic) culture and considering how they work in relation to biblical studies. Finally, I am not
able to resist a moment in which I attempt to trace some postcolonial possibilities out of the present and into the future.

On Postcolonialism

I want to suggest that postcolonialism is closely tied in with postmodernism (not an overly original suggestion, to begin with),
which I characterize in terms of a dialectical conjunction between
globalization and disintegration. This implies a connection
between postmodernism as a cultural phenomenon (its most
common formulation) and as a socio-economic development (at
times this dimension is described as late capitalism). In order to
make this connection I rely upon a Marxist construction of the
Real in which the realm of culture, aesthetics and so on, has a
necessary but complex relationship with political economics.
Rather than proposing a solution, this relationship—normally
designated in terms of base and superstructure—states a problem
that requires innovative thinking. Given this basic formulation,
postmodernism—straddling both base and superstructure—is
understood as an intense dialectical opposition between globalization and disintegration.[1]

The term 'globalization' has made its way into discourses as
diverse as sport, psychoanalysis, anthropology, urban planning,
religion, and of course economics. All are concerned with the way
certain questions and issues in these and other disciplines are
permeating all areas of the globe irrespective of the boundaries of
the nation-state. But it is economics that is the common denomi-
nator, and here globalization means the worldwide dominance,
for the first time, of capitalist modes and relations of production.[2]

1. I have argued this in more detail in 'The Decree of the Watchers:
Globalization, Disintegration and Daniel 4' (unpublished). This issue is pursued, although without the explicit connection between globalization and
disintegration, in Wilson and Dissanayake (1996).
2. A more restrained economic definition comes from Cowhey and

But what is interesting is the way such a global capitalism generates its Other, namely, reification, which is a more philosophical version of disintegration. Reification operates on at least two levels: the exchange of relations between human beings and objects generated in the production process, that is, the relations between inanimate objects are attributed with the nature of those of human beings, and vice versa; and the increasing fragmentation of social life, both in the production process (Taylorization—the breakdown of production into smaller and smaller units and tasks) and outside. On a more economic level, reification becomes commodification, the process whereby not only the products in the market are commodities but everything else is commodified as well. It is under the umbrella of disintegration that I also include both the much-commented-upon postmodern phenomenon of depthlessness or focus on the surface, and the critical-theoretical terminology of difference and heterogeneity—the interest in that which breaks or at least threatens capitalist hegemony—since even this difference turns out to be part of the logic of capitalism itself. The advantage of formulating postmodernism in terms of globalization and disintegration is that it accounts for both the uniqueness of postmodernism and its continuity with earlier phases. The uniqueness arises from the extraordinary intensity and pace of globalization and disintegration under late capitalism, while the continuity recognizes that this is yet another phase in a pattern (capitalism) for which the seeds were sown in the sixteenth century.

The reason for setting postmodernism up in this way is to make the connection with postcolonialism, since postcolonialism is not so much a subset of postmodernism as constitutive of the postmodern moment in the first place. In other words, the intense dialectical opposition of globalization and disintegration shows up most sharply in postcolonialism, leading to the suggestion that this opposition is a determinative feature of postcolonialism as such. A couple of (general) examples will reinforce my point. It

Aronson: '[w]e use globalization to mean that the leading firms rely on foreign markets, on production and competitive assets (such as access to research and development) in other countries, and on global networks (such as the global payments network shared by the leading banks) to accomplish their fundamental business objectives' (1993: 14).

seems that each time the forces of decolonization have arisen—whether in Australia and Canada in the late nineteenth century, Africa and Asia in the mid to late twentieth century—this has become a means for yet more intense colonization. Those places which achieved their status as nation-states in the struggle against their largely European colonizers found themselves under the sway of a more powerful mutation in capitalism in their postcolonial phase. Sadly, this has also been the experience of those nation-states that moved on the impulse of a socialist agenda. This general trend is, then, an example where the disintegration of the old European colonial powers has led to more intense globalization, all of which is part of the logic of capitalism itself. An example that begins from the side of globalization is that of Aboriginal art, whose move to a position of strength in the 1980s and 1990s is due in large part to the interest of the international art market. Here the global market has the effect of raising the importance of a distinct and local cultural form, providing a profile for Aboriginal art that was simply not possible before market interest. Of course, the very object that the international market desires, changes the moment that market makes significant contact with the long tradition of Aboriginal art production.

In their own ways these examples indicate how the patterns of globalization and disintegration—tied in very closely with political economics—have a stark presence in much that goes by the name of 'postcolonialism'. However, there is one final point to be made here, and in this I am indebted to Fredric Jameson (although I want to raise some questions as well). Postcolonialism may be understood as that which arises as part of (while simultaneously becoming definitive of) that phase of capitalism Jameson designates 'late capitalism'. In fact, Jameson has argued in 'Periodizing the 60s' (Jameson 1984) that an important part of the shift into postmodernism is located in the move of certain Third World colonial countries towards independence from their various colonial masters. Yet, while Jameson's thesis is perhaps valid for the area with which he is dealing (the independence movements of the 1950s, 1960s and 1970s), it is not sufficiently aware of the complexity and overdetermination of (post)colonialism itself. While I do not wish to take the line of the editors of *The Empire Writes Back* (Ashcroft, Griffiths, Tiffin 1989)—that all literature

produced from the first moments of European colonialism may
be classified as postcolonial—the limited example of Australia
indicates some of the problems with Jameson's proposal (and
thus any other that would focus on this period as determinative
for postcolonialism).

Australia belongs to a group of white male settler colonies, in
distinction from indigenous or 'non-white' colonies, or at least
places where the European contingent was always a significant but
very powerful minority. It belongs, then, to that exclusive club
that includes the USA, Canada and New Zealand, where the
attempt to kill the indigenous peoples was most systematically
perpetrated. However, despite being, along with Canada and New
Zealand, the site for an earlier wave of decolonization in the later
nineteenth century, the resulting semi-independent status was
established in such a way—framed in a rather hasty and patchwork constitution—as to allow the drive to decolonization to
expend itself while keeping Australia firmly tied into British society and political economics. In this context Australia itself became
a minor colonial nation in the South Pacific, exercising its pater-
nal care over a number of small islands and Papua New Guinea.
In fact, Australia's involvement with the decolonizing moves of
the decades following the Second World War lay in Papua New
Guinea, which was 'granted' independence on 16 September
1975.

What is significant (and appalling) about the Australian situation is how smoothly a penal settlement with its own subordinate
status in relation to the colonial metropolis of London (a
dystopian view) should at the same time be understood and
understand itself to be a force for colonization over the land and
its Aboriginal people (for settlers a 'utopian' view, emphasizing
wealth and a regenerated social order). The British settlement of
1788 was, in other words, both a subject of and an agent of colonialism, the relations between indigenous peoples and settlers
overlaid with the relations between England and the settlers
(Fuery 1993: 196). Australia also has a claim to the unique status
of beginning its colonial history as a prison, 'a gulag for "excess"
victims of the Industrial Revolution', to quote Meaghan Morris,
which 'went through genocide and ethnocide and gynocide to
pioneer hyper-discreet forms of apartheid and race management

through genetic engineering' (Morris 1992: 477). This prison was both overwhelmingly male and extraordinarily brutal.

Yet I have reverted to a myth of origins by invoking the founding story of non-indigenous settlement in Australia. In order to correct this I want to pick up more explicitly the opposition between globalization and disintegration, in particular the political direction of Australia in the 1990s. As a sort of final chapter in the colonial history of Australia, there is an increasing consensus across political parties and the populace that Australia should move towards becoming a republic by 2001, one hundred years after the establishment of the Australian nation-state, and one year after the Sydney Olympics, which will conveniently generate their own nationalistic fervour. This is, at first appearance, a chronically outdated movement, for the drive to nation-states characteristic of earlier capitalism is to all intents and purposes over. I would suggest that this is not so strange as it seems once the earlier opposition of globalization and disintegration is brought to bear: although the dialectically opposed Balkanization of Europe and the process to a European superstate may appear to be unrelated, it is of the same type as Australia's assertion of republican status in a world increasingly overrun by multinational companies. As Australia is belatedly wired into an integrated and global electronic/economic communications system, the older colonial dependencies on Britain and then more recently on the USA begin to slip away before the power of multinational capital with its integrated media/market. The disintegration of a former colonial hegemony in Australia—marked among other things by the breakdown of an Anglo-Celtic culture, and the increasing number of people from Asia and the Pacific—sees a more intense globalization as everything that is diverse and distinct, including Australian Aboriginal life and belief, is drawn up into the vortex of a global postmodern culture and market.

Despite all of this, I want to reinforce a need for considerable trepidation and hesitancy in any move into postcolonial theory, particularly in the light of Anne McClintock's bitter critique of the term and the associations trailing along behind it.

> While admittedly another p-c word, 'post-colonialism' is arguably more palatable and less foreign-sounding to sceptical deans than 'Third World Studies'. It also has a less accusatory ring than

'Studies in Neo-colonialism', say, or 'Fighting Two Colonialisms'. It
is more global, and less fuddy-duddy, than 'Commonwealth Studies'. The term borrows, moreover, on the dazzling marketing success of the term 'post-modernism'. As the organizing rubric of an
emerging field of disciplinary studies and an archive of knowledge,
the term 'post-colonialism' makes possible the marketing of a
whole new generation of panels, articles, books and courses
(McClintock 1993: 299).

Not only is there some dread or anxiety about the term on my
part, but I have also imposed a self-limitation on my discussion of
postcolonialism to Australia. However, in concluding, I want to
make one observation, and that is that postcolonialism itself par-
takes of a deeper pattern of periodization which seems to afflict
our thinking. For reasons that need to be considered in detail
somewhere else, it seems to me that we have two options within
our present intellectual and social horizon. The first is to attempt
some organization of history into distinct periods which may be
identified according to sets of features which mark them off from
other periods which will then have their own distinct features.
The second option is to argue that history is far too complex to
periodize in any meaningful sense. Postcolonialism falls clearly
within the orbit of periodization, being in this sense that which
comes after the era of (capitalist) colonialism.

Antipodean Biblical Studies

What, then, are the implications and possibilities for biblical studies, particularly in Australia? Alongside a desire to trace the development of biblical studies in Australia—which has in some sense
always been a colonial endeavour—I want to exploit some images
of Australia in order to suggest the ways postcolonial biblical
studies might offer the promise of an alternative to, or may even
undermine, the forms of Euro-American biblical criticism dominant until now. That there is something utopian about this I see
no need to hide. The images of which I write are in fact clichés of
the white settler community in Australia. In using these clichés I
run the risk of misrepresentation, but such a risk seems worthwhile in the pursuit of the ideological constructs that determine
the nature of biblical scholarship, if not the intellectual life in
Australia in general, with all its limits and possibilities (the notion

of misrepresentation is itself troubled, since it assumes that a realistic representation of what goes on is possible in the first place). My three images or clichés are cultural hierarchy, cultural cringe and the tyranny of distance.

I borrow 'cultural hierarchy' from John Docker, who in his turn develops it from Frantz Fanon's 'hierarchy of values'. It denotes a scaled inferiority in which the indigenous, Aboriginal culture is devalued by the colonial settlers, whose culture is itself understood to be inferior to the colonial centre. Such a scaled approach does not deal sufficiently with either Aboriginal or imperial cultures, lying at either extreme of the scale, but its focus is the central term—white settler culture—which is depicted as a conflictual site, a place of 'profound psychological disturbance, at once guilty of enforcing inferiority on others, and haunted by self-doubt and self-contempt before the metropolitan culture's necessary superiority' (Docker 1995: 443). This is ultimately a colonial self-perception, but such a hierarchy continues to characterize the way many intellectuals function: any contributions from Aboriginal or Koori people, from students through to established writers, are measured and often dismissed on the basis of metropolitan-derived academic standards. From the other direction, Australian biblical scholars remain 'haunted by self-doubt and contempt' (Docker 1995: 443) before the juggernauts of European and North American biblical studies.

It is only a small step from cultural hierarchy to 'cultural cringe'—an almost physical repulsion that bearers of metropolitan or imperial culture feel in the face of anything that champions a distinctly Australian identity or flavour, more often than not in the realm of popular or mass culture. Anything that has a distinctly 'ocker' tone, that speaks with a strong drawl, that devotes itself to Australian derivations of country-and-western or folk material, that plays upon myths of the (male) larrikin or bushman, and that celebrates the focus on sport and leisure, becomes an object of sophisticated derision and avoidance. That this also has strong class dimensions—especially in a country that at times lays claim to being a classless society—should not be forgotten. Manifestations of cultural cringe are found with those who place themselves in the upper middle class of Australian society, although even here jingoistic nationalism has made strong inroads. Further, there are those who either visit or migrate to Australia from the decayed colonial centres of Europe, arriving with an assumed superiority of European culture over against the derived colonial culture of Australia. All of this is then reinforced by the popularity of the crassest of Australian television programs, particularly soap operas like *Home and Away* in the late 1980s and 1990s, in the place termed 'home' (England) by the majority of an older generation of white settlers. The very shoddiness of the programs reinforces the sense of cultural superiority that is assumed from the European side.

Another group for whom cultural cringe has been a determining force is of course the intellectuals who by and large arrived in Australia from Europe for a shorter or longer term (on this, see below). The intellectual dimensions of cultural cringe remain very strong even for contemporary 'home grown' intellectuals, since the prestige of publication at a press in Europe or the USA far outweighs that of an Australian press, and participation in conferences based in the northern hemisphere is far more desirable than those in the Australian region. I must confess my own somewhat unavoidable guilt in expressions of cultural cringe, particularly when theology or biblical studies in Australia lays claim to a nationalistic or patriotic agenda, but I will return to this.

The 'tyranny of distance'—a 'cliché of Australian pop historiography' (Morris 1988: 165)—is a phrase still encountered at times in the 1990s in Australia. Coined by Geoffrey Blainey in 1966, the term continues to designate the absence of Europe (and more recently North America) on the visible landscape. Yet it has a double reference: 'tyranny of distance' referred not only to the relation between Europe and the coastal cities of Australia, but to the relation between those coastal cities and the arid interior, that is, the phrase referred to the size of a largely desert land itself. All the same, today it is usually dredged up in order to be thrown back into the past as a state which no longer holds due to the wonders of travel and communications technology. This manoeuvre often evokes mixed images and emotions: of recoil at crude and tough conditions at a pioneer station at the edge of the world (last stop, apart from New Zealand perhaps, on the way to the Antarctic), of nostalgia for a time of braver men, of thankfulness for Australia's belated incorporation into media society. For biblical (and other) scholars such a tyranny basically referred to the three months or more it took for passage by boat from Australia to England, Scotland, Wales or Ireland—the commercial run which ensured Australia's place in the British Empire. This meant, of course, that for any scholar travelling 'home' in a sabbatical year half of the time was spent in transit. Even if the travel seems to have been two-way, in terms of resources for academic appointments the flow was overwhelmingly from the 'old country' to Australian institutions. To be sure, a few journeyed in reverse, invariably not to return as they became comfortable expatriates (more recently and well known in biblical studies are John O'Neill, Francis Andersen and David Clines). Yet the long colonial tradition of academic reproduction in Australia lay in the expectation that boats would continue disgorging scholars, while from the English side a placement in a colony like Australia or Canada might fall into an acceptable academic career pattern. Not that these were all second rate or even useless, but by and large the better scholars did not choose the colonies, except perhaps some younger scholars out for quick advancement and the chance for some publications before returning home in triumph. In those areas where biblical scholars were required—the training institutes of the various churches—the assumption until the 1960s (and beyond in some cases) was that selection/search committees invariably looked 'home' for replacements.

Nevertheless, the imperial legacy was neither resolutely negative (as in the famous 'What have the Romans done for us?' sequence in *The Life of Brian*) nor were biblical scholars always shown the greatest hospitality. In all of the colonial period perhaps the marker of a deeper ambivalence was a predilection for heresy trials against the occasional English and Scottish biblical scholar. Not only was the 'churchman' Charles Strong accused of heresy—his Melbourne congregation left the Presbyterians and formed an independent church—but in the 1930s the reasonably well-published New Testament scholar Samuel Angus was accused of heresy, although never finally convicted. His sin was the advocacy of classical Christian liberalism (see Emilsen 1991). In a huge time warp that fits better in a science fiction novel, a heresy charge was upheld in 1992 against another New Testament scholar who came from Scotland in 1990 to become the head of

St Andrews College at Sydney University. Although it seemed to be the fundamentalist rump of a continuing Presbyterian Church charging a conventionally liberal Peter Cameron, the language of anti-colonialism ran strongly in the whole procedure.

A number of other factors influence the ideological make-up of academics in Australia, apart from (yet structurally related to) those which are integral to their situation in regard to class (relations of production) and political economics (mode of production). Among the former should be included a relative absence of intellectual stimulus and lack of academic resources (both closely tied in with tyrannical distance), the relatively small number of academics as a whole (especially biblical scholars among whom potential job movements are often known well in advance), a wide anti-intellectualism in Australian society in response to which intellectuals prefer to travel incognito in transit from one safe house to another, and a virtual absence of the pressure to publish, particularly within the seminary or college system. However, what is interesting to note here is a patchwork professionalization and 'Americanization' of academic life (to borrow a term from Ahmad in regard to India [Ahmad 1992: 278-81]), in which the pressure for higher degrees, conference hunting and professional publication is beginning to make inroads into biblical and theological studies, although there are plenty of academics who hold onto the older tradition of being of service to the church before being intellectuals and scholars. These elements should be related to the nature of institutional life, in which the various churches and the state have often arranged compromise deals in both funding and control (most recently the state-funded Australian Catholic University, but also state allowances for students at the various theological colleges), and where the universities have overwhelmingly been run by the state, flirting occasionally with the old 'queen', theology, and more recently religious studies. Yet even in the newer religious studies programs which cling to the edge of existence biblical scholars struggle to find a place, except perhaps under cover, researching in biblical studies while teaching in other areas of religious studies.

If cultural hierarchy, cultural cringe and the tyranny of distance go some way towards characterizing the ideological context for biblical scholarship in Australia, then I want to suggest that there have been, until and into the postmodern/postcolonial era, three major possibilities for the pursuit of biblical studies—emulation, nationalism and positive unoriginality. For (biblical) scholars in places outside the superstates the dominant option in the past has been emulation of the work done in the metropolitan centres from which those scholars inevitably came (for Australia this was for so long England, Scotland, even Ireland for Roman Catholic scholars). The intensity of the drive to emulate metropolitan scholarship seems inversely related to the distance from the metropolitan centres: emulation seemed to be the appropriate response to the tyranny of distance. Those disgorged by the boats mentioned earlier worked hard to emulate the scholarship and teaching of their own source, thereby attempting to erase their colonial presence in any teaching or writing they might undertake. Part of this of course was due to the training those scholars received before arriving in Australia and, in fact, it is only in the last two generations that biblical scholars have trained in Australia, or returned after study and work overseas (e.g. Norman Habel in Adelaide or Mark Brett in Melbourne). This is a rather ambivalent change, since although there is an increasing trend to Australian-born incumbents who have completed Australian degrees, the pressure remains for intending scholars to procure graduate degrees in North America or the UK and then return to take up posts in Australia itself, if they are not in the meantime drawn into the academic market place of these larger metropolitan centres. The paradox here is that with an increasing trend to a complete Australian cycle of academic life there is a simultaneous increase in insularity, with distinct marks of lack of international contact.

The change towards Australian-bred biblical scholars has, however, led to the flowering of the second option I noted above—nationalism—although it has had a sporadic existence alongside the stronger tendency to emulation. Although stemming politically and socially from the 1890s—the drive towards semi-independent status in relation to the colonial power of Britain resulted in the compromise deal of the federated Australian commonwealth of 1901—and finding more recent life with the drive to become a Republic by 2001, the nationalist option pre-

sents a curious bind for biblical scholarship. For many scholars it
seems to be the only way to avoid what is increasingly regarded as
the undesirable practice of metropolitan emulation, of the
encroachment of the global system of scholarly dominance. By
'nationalist' I refer to intense interest in 'contextual' issues, in
that which has a uniquely Australian feel to it; all of which is most
often expressed in terms of Australian publishing, scholars,
appointment and content, but it rarely includes Aboriginal discourses and mostly assumes that the adjective 'Australian' is an
unambiguous term in itself. The connections between this move
in (biblical) scholarship and the opposition between globalization
and disintegration that I noted above in regard to Australia's own
(post)colonial history should not be missed, but there are some
interesting twists within a nationalist emphasis. To begin with, the
distinctness of Australian forms of academic produce is often presented as a resistance to 'American' influence, specifically that of
the USA. The feeling here is that the truly global cultural forces
are those which stem from the USA—most notably in Hollywood
films, television programming, McDonald's, Coke, Pepsi, and so
on. Yet the resistance to these all-too-persistent influences is often
cast in Anglophile terms, asserting those values which were the
hallmark of emulation of the metropolitan centres. One final twist
here is that the issues of scholarly value often operate with the
canonical, metropolitan assumptions of the metropolitan centres
themselves: thus, success depends upon showing such centres that
something good can in fact come out of Australia, despite contrary expectations.

Yet, as I have argued above, the increasing assertion of a
national identity is part of the dynamic of globalization itself: the
desire to be distinct is generated in response to the inexorable
drive to economic and cultural uniformity. And then in the very
response to globalization, at the point where one feels a genuine
oppositional move has been made, globalization shows through
even more strongly. I am thinking here of the way particular
ethnic, local and national quirks become the stuff of global fashion and interest—Australian accents and films, Aboriginal art and
literature, to name a few more notable examples. The key term
here that is closely related to the national but generates its own
logic is the 'exotic', a term redolent with older colonial associa-

tions. The attraction is that there is something distinctly South-East Asian or South Pacific about Australia and its location, yet its dominant culture is Western and language English—something both familiar and strange. (This 'exotic' status operates a little like certain forms of global tourism which may be defined by the internally contradictory need to avoid being touristic by seeking precisely those areas not frequented by [too many] tourists.) Thus, biblical studies in Australia may be said to be truly 'national' when it digs deep into that which is distinct or exotic about the place itself. As a colonial construct, the exotic appeal is what drew at least some scholars to Australian appointments in the first place, and then kept them there for a lifetime of work. And it seems that Australia's exotic status may pay some postcolonial dividends, with its very distance and poverty of intellectual life being that which attracts those who have traditionally had a surfeit of accessibility and intellectual stimulus. All of this points finally to the deeply conflicted yet relentless logic of a globalization which inevitably absorbs the very particularities of a local situation: one by one the local quirks and oddities are put on public display where they quickly lose their exotic status and become humdrum.

A third option—positive unoriginality—has played an ambiguous role in biblical scholarship in this part of the world. In using the phrase 'positive unoriginality' I want to designate the troubled place of modernism (as both a term within biblical scholarship and as a designation of a cultural period) on the Australian scene. As the Australian cultural critic, Meaghan Morris, has argued (1990: 10-11), modernism in Australia, at least in the realms of architecture and cultural theory, has rarely been driven by slogans of the *novum*—innovation, originality, future, rupture, unknown, and so on. Whatever was 'modern' was understood 'as a *known history*, something which has *already happened elsewhere*, and which is to be reproduced, mechanically or otherwise, with a local content' (Morris 1990: 11). The introduction of modernism, then, was more a case of catching up with metropolitan centres in a perpetual time lag, and by the time they arrived there was a distinctly archaic feel to modernist cultural artifacts. And biblical studies shows this up in a rather remarkable fashion, modernist or liberal methods of biblical study arriving late and with considerable suspicion in the person of Samuel Angus, Professor of New Testament at the Presbyterian Theological Hall at Sydney University in the earlier part of the twentieth century. Vilified and idolized in his lifetime, the near-martyr status granted Angus after his death ensured that the modernist currents of biblical and theological scholarship from the turn of the century that he embodied carried on within sections of the Protestant churches well into the 1960s and 1970s. But this is not the only use of 'positive unoriginality': here my debts are to a study of the film *Crocodile Dundee* by Meaghan Morris. The film is for Morris 'a post-*colonial* comedy of survival' (Morris 1988: 244), enabled by a clever positioning in relation to the American film market and Hollywood itself. Neither original nor mere copy, the film pursues a 'positive unoriginality', a process of copying which persistently alters the 'original' so that it comes out the worse for the imitation (for example, Davy Crockett is the worse for the comparison). But the activity is reciprocal, since the various items of Australia's own ideological make-up undergo a similar process of belittlement—the bushman, aboriginality, the outback, mateship, larrikinism, masculinism. This cultural strategy appeals most to me for a possible mode of postcolonial biblical studies, although I will want to suggest some shortfalls as well as the need to go beyond it.

The most appealing dimension of this sort of positive unoriginality lies in the disavowal of the need to take the international currents of biblical scholarship with complete seriousness. There is, in other words, a rather welcome mockery or jocularity about the endeavour—what counts in the end is a good beer and a few jokes, and anyone who takes things too seriously is either a nerd or a dag.[3] Such a positive unoriginality means not only a process of what Marxists would call 'demystification'—the need continually to call the bluff on reactionary and conservative ideological formations (in other words, crap detection)—but also an appropriation of whatever methodological means are provided on the global theoretical market (this is the 'unoriginal' bit) and the use of such methods for more intense studies of biblical texts in conjunction with local textual artifacts (this is the positive bit). The models I would suggest here are those of Sreten Bozic and

3. 'Dag', originally dried dung on sheep's wool, but later carrying a sense comparable to nerd, originated in New Zealand.

Mudrooroo Narogin. Both embody the contradiction character-istic of postcolonialism as such,[4] since both have slippery and uncertain identities (most debate has in fact focused, not unex-pectedly, on questions of authenticity and identity). Mudrooroo, either an African American or Nyoongah Aboriginal, brings about a conjunction between Aboriginal forms and content and those of European and Indian background (Mudrooroo Narogin Nyoon-gah 1979; 1983; 1987; 1991; 1992; 1993). Sreten Bozic, a Serbian immigrant, amateur anthropological fieldworker, and writer of an astounding series of poems, short stories and novels—especially the 'nuclear trilogy' of *Walg* (1986), *Karan* (1986) and *Gabo Djara* (1988)—writes as the Aboriginal, Banumbir Wongar, and at times as a woman. Not only is each novel a 'site of contestation between European and Aboriginal narratives' (Connor and Matthews 1989: 719) and between genders, but each one also problematizes the status of such distinctions (see Gunew 1993; Boer 1997). Both Bozic and Mudrooroo offer unique specimens to an international market by means of the tools provided by globalization.

However, I want to return to my characterization of postcolo-nialism in terms of globalization and disintegration and argue that the distinct nature of any area, or of any local tradition, mode of interpretation or group of scholars is enabled by the means made available internationally by the globalization of academic life. Thus, for instance, Meaghan Morris, Australia's foremost cultural critic,[5] deals with Australian popular culture in terms of French and American theories of culture which are no longer particularly French or American but transnational. From biblical and theological studies comes the example of *Freedom and Entrap-ment*, a collection of essays on Australian feminism and theology edited by the Melbourne New Testament scholar Dorothy Lee,[6] as well as Maryanne Confoy and Joan Nowotny (1995), but with a foreword by Elisabeth Schüssler Fiorenza. The tension I have been pursuing comes out most sharply in the paper 'Not Yet

---

4.   Ashcroft, Griffiths and Tiffin would prefer hybridity as 'the primary characteristic of all post-colonial texts' (1989: 185).

5.   For a fuller treatment of Morris's work see my 'Preaching Dungog'.

6.   In fact, the percentage of women teaching biblical studies in Australia is quite high, especially in New Testament, although this must be balanced by the small number of those teaching in biblical studies as a whole.

Tiddas', by Anne Pattel-Gray (1995), an Aboriginal activist and religious thinker about whom the Romanian-born Fiorenza writes in proper postcolonial form. For Schüssler Fiorenza, an Aboriginal woman writing on theology from Australia is precisely where the future for biblical studies, the academy and the church lies. Yet in order to make her intervention in the relatively small scene of Australian religious and theological feminism, Pattel-Gray makes use of the developments in womanist work in North America, appropriating in her turn its racial and class dimensions for an Australian situation.

Indeed, it would be possible to push the seeds of this contradiction back into colonialism proper, when many of the trajectories, such as Christianity itself, were set on their way to end up in the distinctive cultural, theological and biblical contributions from places outside the former metropolitan centers (see the Asian examples in Sugirtharajah 1993: 54-63). For biblical studies all of this means not merely an appropriation by a relentlessly globalizing scholarship but also the chance to adapt to a 'critical regionalism' (the phrase is from architecture; see Frampton 1983) the tools of postmodern and postcolonial discourse in order to provide interpretations from the local situation which begin, homeopathically, to resist and undermine the logic of those instruments. Biblical studies in Australia may then be able to offer its own unique specimens to an international market by means of the very tools that such a global situation supplies.

Conclusion

Yet it seems to me that a homeopathic solution is finally not enough, although the assumption that a solution is required at all will begin to indicate the direction I want to take in this final section. For all the attraction and promise of the proposals I have sketched out in terms of positive unoriginality, it is still part of a process: the various possibilities of a postcolonial biblical criticism need to be sketched out in some more detail, although, like any projection of future possibilities, it is fraught with the usual difficulties. Here I want to be, in other words, unashamedly prescriptive.

Any discussion of such future possibilities in Australia, and for

that matter in most other places, needs to begin with an awareness of the institutional matrix within which biblical studies is
done and might be done. My initial debts here are, of course, to
Foucault, but I also want to draw upon a line of thought more
directly in the Marxist tradition, namely, that of Louis Althusser,
who made the point in what is now a very influential essay that
our educational institutions function as major tools in the control
and direction of thought and practice in our societies. Along with
some other institutions, such as government, the police, the
armed forces, the judicial system, and the medical establishment,
both educational facilities and religion are labelled 'ideological
state apparatuses' in the essay 'Ideology and Ideological State
Apparatuses (Notes towards an Investigation)' (Althusser 1971:
121-73; 1984: 1-60). In other words, they serve a crucial function
in the ideological formation—understood by Althusser as the
complex ways in which individuals make sense of their relation to
the wider social whole—of people in society. Althusser does not
have in mind a crude sort of brainwashing, but rather a more
ambiguous production of the ideas, stories, arguments and so on
which are crucial for social existence (ideology thus shifts from its
more traditional negative associations). In this context a battle is
fought between different classes for ideological control with
whatever means are available. And this is how I would like to
understand educational institutions such as the theological college in Australia: that they are sites of ideological conflict, of
tension and difference, which have their source only partially in
the variety of theological options at work in the church today and
more widely in the class tensions and economic constraints of
Australia and overseas. They are sites therefore in which the dominant forms of ideology are most often assumed but where others
are fought over and sometimes challenged: this means that religion becomes one of the languages in which social conflict is
undertaken, and the numerous tensions within the church might
be fruitfully read in this way.

   An additional factor concerning the nature of theological and
other educational institutions in Australia is the strong government presence over the 1980s and 1990s, with a specific agenda
for the funding control of education and the desire to generate
an educated workforce. Yet biblical studies is nearly without

exception taught in the college or seminary situation. Any connection with universities comes through college personnel teaching occasional university courses or by mutual arrangements
between colleges and universities (such as Parkin-Wesley College
and Flinders University in Adelaide, the Brisbane College of Theology and Griffith University in Brisbane). Even in such mutual
arrangements, the dominant context of teaching is the college.[7]
Thus, the development of any postcolonial program for biblical
studies will need to take such an institutional situation into
account.

Before considering some modes of disrupting the dominant
ways of studying the Bible, I need to connect Althusser's notion of
ideological state apparatuses with political economics. For
Althusser, the institutions of education and the church play a
crucial role in being the locus of ideological battles concerning
capitalism itself, since, although they may derive from other
modes of production such as feudalism, they are very much part
of the capitalist economic order. They are the institutions upon
which, finally, capitalism continues to depend for its own ideological survival. This may take more direct forms, such as the elaboration of the various positions and possibilities of liberalism, or
indirect forms, such as the strengthening of capitalism through
the systematic criticism that these institutions may develop.
Despite the appropriate checks to curtail criticism that cannot be
incorporated, every now and then the critical capacity of institutions overflows the boundaries and becomes a source of revolutionary unrest—the prime example here of course is the movement of student insurrection in Paris in May 1968. All of this
requires the gradual development and build-up of a 'culture' of
alternative ways of thinking and acting, and it is this that I would

7.   A significant signal of this bifurcation is the refusal in 1996 of the
federal government's Department for Education, Employment and Training
to accept the application from the Melbourne College of Divinity for funding. It is true that a couple of people in universities research in biblical studies, but do not teach in it (Majella Franzman at the University of New England, and Professor Frank Maloney of the Australian Catholic University);
this situation of course changes with personnel. The exception in the
University of Queensland's religion department only reinforces my general
point of a significant gulf.

like to take up in my proposals for the promise of postcolonial biblical criticism.

Biblical studies is itself a subset of religion, which belongs to the superstructure of the totality of society, sharing that space with art, culture, philosophy, politics and ideology (although this latter term is all-encompassing); it is then dependent upon the economic forms and social relations of that society, yet it may also anticipate possible future forms of social and economic organization. Biblical studies has an ambiguous role in all of this, since the Bible has played a constitutive role in the development of 'Western' culture, which itself has moved through the Roman Empire and feudal Europe into capitalism, where Christianity seems to have foundered and taken on a more marginalized status.

With this model in mind, there are, it seems to me, two possibilities for the ways postcolonial biblical studies may disrupt conventional or metropolitan ways of studying the Bible. The first owes its debts to the important work of Ernesto Laclau and Chantal Mouffe, *Hegemony and Socialist Strategy*. In their efforts to think through the political implications of poststructuralism and a more encompassing postmodernism, they theorize concerning the profoundly postmodern development of a host of small political pressure groups, normally designated with the term 'micropolitics' and engaging in political practices that no longer follow older class lines. Mouffe and Laclau also want to reshape Gramsci's notion of hegemony, and they do so by developing an anti-essentialist ideological framework for this new micropolitics, whose various groups will eventually move into alliances based on their drive for a radical equality. Although there are some problems in losing the Marxist base for such equality—the universalization of wage labour and of the commodity form (see Jameson 1991: 319; Larsen 1990 for a stronger critique)—it seems to me that there is some initial promise for the possibilities of postcolonial biblical studies. Of course, I would like to recover the role of class which begins to disappear in the work of Mouffe and Laclau, since the danger of much reflection about the new social movements relies on the idea that the older class politics have dissipated in the new dispensation (rather, the older configurations of class and politics have been redistributed with the new global reorganization of

capital and its technologies). Yet, as Jameson reminds the perse-
vering reader, all of these groups in the micro-political arena,
including those newly identified, owe their 'ultimate systemic
condition of possibility' (1991: 325) to late capitalism. It is within
this context that any alternative possibilities for postcolonial forms
of biblical criticism must situate themselves, although I am
sufficiently a Marxist to hold that the very possibility of overturning a dominant system comes in part from the logic of that system
itself. I write 'in part', since not all the processes of breakdown are
the result of internal contradictions; some oppositional currents
may come from 'outside' the economic system and threaten to
disrupt its desire for business as usual. This seems particularly per-
tinent to micro-groups within postcolonialism, who remain both
constitutive of postmodern capitalism as such and yet come from
'beyond' to challenge such an economic system. This may be the
place for Aboriginal contributions to biblical studies, or indigenous possibilities in other parts of the globe, although I want to
avoid the dangers of both 'idealization' and 'appropriation' that
David Spurr has identified as basic to the colonial agenda (see
especially Spurr 1993: 28-42, 125-40). In the end I am not sure
that anything can come any longer from 'outside' late capitalism,
so that any forms of resistance, in which indigenous people are
sure to play a part, need to come from elsewhere. Biblical critics
may be identified as yet another political and social grouping in
the micro-political territory of late capitalism, yet an oppositional
stand from biblical critics in postcolonial situations would seem to
be possible only within the dynamic of capitalism itself.

However, even the suggestions of Laclau and Mouffe do not
seem to me to go far enough, particularly with the peculiarly inef-
fectual nature of much small-group politics—insofar as one's
desire is for permanent radical change. It seems to me that the
greatest promise here lies with the work of Aijaz Ahmad, who
articulates a distinct place for a Marxist postcolonial praxis. It is
not so much the devastating critique of Third-Worldism, or the
three worlds theory as such, nor his clarifications of Marx's writings on India or the question of Indian literature, nor his critical
engagements with the work of Fredric Jameson, Edward Said and
Salman Rushdie, that I want to focus on here, but rather the
argument that the only viable form of political and social opposi-

tion in this present world comes from socialism. This of course identifies Aijaz as a relatively orthodox Marxist, but it also signals something about India itself that is often forgotten in the heavily European focus of much Marxist work, namely, the long experience of Marxist government within a secular, democratic state. I am thinking here of the viability of the Marxist governments of Kerala and West Bengal that have provided a pattern of economic and social reform that has ensured them a firm electoral base over many years. The difference here, in comparison to Western Europe, North America and countries such as Australia (where Fred Patterson remains the only Communist Party candidate to be elected to a state Government—that of Queensland), is that the experience of elected government has provided a practical political base for significant theoretical reflection.

It is from this context that Ahmad sounds most strongly the old Marxist argument that in the present historical conjunction— global capitalism—the only coherent alternative remains socialism. Moving from the point that the great majority of former colonial countries cannot make the transition to a fully fledged capitalism of the European type, since they have no external, imperial, resources to exploit, he argues:

> This structural inability of capitalism to provide for the vast majority of the populations which it has sucked into its own dominion constitutes the basic, incurable flaw in the system as a whole... Negation of this contradiction can come only from outside the terms of this system as such, because the backwardness of the backward capitalist countries, hence the poverty of the majority of the world's population, cannot be undone except through a complete redistribution of wealth and an altogether different structuring of productions and consumptions on a global scale, among classes, regions, countries and continents of the world. Socialism is the determinate name for this negation of capitalism's fundamental, systemic contradictions and cruelties (1992: 316).

And the primary object of socialist resistance is precisely those backward economic formations, those who have been colonized and are now belatedly included in full-blown capitalism only to be denied inclusion. This is where, it seems to me, the oppositional dimensions of postcolonialism may be found.

But how can biblical studies be a part of all this? I want to pick up Fredric Jameson's suggestion that culture—of which biblical studies is a part (and in the construction of 'Western' culture it has played a constitutive role)—may also be *anticipatory* as well as determined by economic formations, that the superstructure may provide a glimpse of better possibilities. What is required, then, is the development and improvement of a Marxist or socialist culture, of the discussion, debate and reflection on Marxism within the context of capitalism itself (of which Marxism remains the most potent interpreter), as well as the production of art, literature, film, music and so on that is properly oppositional, and a full Marxist criticism that may interpret all that has gone before. It is to the ongoing construction of such a culture that biblical criticism may contribute, so that when the moment arrives, biblical criticism may not be found wanting. If I connect this with Ahmad's argument concerning the locus of oppositional socialist practice—those areas that have been and are on the receiving end of capitalist imperialism—then a biblical criticism from a postcolonial space and perspective may find a truly disruptive role.

It seems to me, then, that the most (or should I say 'the only'?) viable mode of destabilizing, disrupting and finally replacing hegemonic, imperial, biblical scholarship is one that seeks to be part of the construction of a culture that anticipates the end of the capitalist social and economic organization that is part and parcel of such a hegemony. Any seriously seditious postcolonial biblical studies needs to make an acquaintance with socialism, in its areas of Marxist political and economic theory and practice, but especially the rich tradition of Marxist literary theory and criticism. For it is here that a truly oppositional discourse may be found.

BIBLIOGRAPHY

Ahmad, Aijaz
    1992   *In Theory: Classes, Nations, Literatures* (London: Verso).
Althusser, Louis
    1971   *Lenin and Philosophy and Other Essays* (trans. Ben Brewster; London: New Left Books).
    1984   *Essays on Ideology* (London: Verso).
Ashcroft, Bill, Gareth Griffiths and Helen Tiffin (eds.)
    1989   *The Empire Writes Back: Theory and Practice in Postcolonial Literature* (London: Routledge & Kegan Paul).

Boer, Roland
    1996a   'Preaching Dungog: The Australian Rural Parish as a Site for Cultural Criticism', *Uniting Church Studies* 1 (2): 25-46.
    1996b   'The Decree of the Watchers: Globalization, Disintegration and Daniel 4', unpublished paper.
    1996c   'Green Ants and Gibeonites: B. Wongar, Joshua 9 and Some Problems of Postcolonialism', *Semeia* 75: 129-52.

Connor, Michael, and David Matthews
    1989   'In the Tracks of the Reader, in the Tracks of B. Wongar', *Meanjin* 48 (4): 713-21.

Cowhey, Peter F., and Jonathan D. Aronson
    1993   *Managing the World Economy: The Consequences of Corporate Alliances* (New York: Council on Foreign Relations).

Docker, John
    1995   'The Neocolonial Assumption in University Teaching of English', in Bill Ashcroft, Gareth Griffiths and Helen Tiffin (eds.), *The Post-Colonial Studies Reader* (London: Routledge & Kegan Paul): 443-46.

Emilsen, Susan
    1991   *A Whiff of Heresy: Samuel Angus and the Presbyterian Church in New South Wales* (Sydney: University of New South Wales Press).

Frampton, Kenneth
    1983   'Towards a Critical Regionalism: Six Points for an Architecture of Resistance', in Hal Foster (ed.), *The Anti-Aesthetic: Essays on Postmodern Culture* (Port Townsend, Washington: Bay Press): 16-30.

Fuery, Patrick
    1993   'Prisoners and Spiders Surrounded by Signs: Postmodernism and the Postcolonial Gaze in Contemporary Australian Culture', in John White (ed.), *Recasting the World: Writing after Colonialism* (Baltimore: The Johns Hopkins University Press): 190-207.

Gunew, Sneja
    1993   'Culture, Gender and Author-Function: "Wongar's" *Walg*', in John Frow and Meaghan Morris (eds.), *Australian Cultural Studies: A Reader* (Sydney: Allen & Unwin): 3-14.

Jameson, Fredric
    1984   'Periodizing the 60s', in Sohnya Sayres *et al.* (eds.), *The 60s without Apology* (Social Text 3.3–4.1; Minneapolis: University of Minnesota Press): 178-209.
    1991   *Postmodernism, or, the Cultural Logic of Late Capitalism* (Durham, NC: Duke University Press).

Laclau, Ernesto, and Chantal Mouffe
    1985   *Hegemony and Socialist Strategy: Towards a Radical Democratic Politics* (London: Verso).

Larsen, Neil
    1990   'Postmodernism and Imperialism: Theory and Politics in Latin America', in *Postmodern Culture* (e-journal: http://jefferson.village.virginia.edu/pmc/contents.all.html; 1 [1], September).

Lee, Dorothy A., Maryanne Confoy, and Joan Nowotny (eds.)
    1995   *Freedom and Entrapment: Women Thinking Theology* (North Blackburn:
                Dove).
McClintock, Anne
    1993   'The Angel of Progress: Pitfalls of the Term "Post-colonialism" ', in
                Patrick Williams and Laura Chrisman (eds.), *Colonial Discourse and
                Post-colonial Theory: A Reader* (Hemel Hempstead: Harvester Wheat-
                sheaf): 291-304.
Morris, Meaghan
    1988   *The Pirate's Fiancée: Feminism, Reading, Postmodernism* (London: Verso).
    1990   'Metamorphoses at Sydney Tower', *New Formations* 11: 5-18.
    1992   ' "On the Beach" ', in Lawrence Grossberg, Cary Nelson and Paula
                A. Treichler (eds.), *Cultural Studies* (London: Routledge & Kegan
                Paul): 450-78.
Mudrooroo Narogin Nyoongah
    1979   *Wild Cat Falling* (Sydney: Angus & Robertson).
    1983   *Doctor Wooredy's Prescription for Enduring the Ending of the World*
                (Melbourne: Hyland House).
    1987   *Long Live Sandawarra* (Melbourne: Hyland House).
    1991   *The Garden of Gethsemane: Poems from the Lost Decade* (South Yarra,
                Victoria: Hyland House).
    1992   *Wild Cat Screaming* (Sydney: Angus & Robertson).
    1993   *The Kwinkan* (Pymble, NSW: Angus & Robertson).
Pattel-Gray, Anne
    1995   'Not Yet Tiddas: An Aboriginal Womanist Critique of Australian
                Church Feminism', in Maryanne Confoy, Dorothy A. Lee and Joan
                Nowotny (eds.), *Freedom and Entrapment: Women Thinking Theology*
                (North Blackburn: Dove): 165-92.
Spurr, David
    1993   *The Rhetoric of Empire: Colonial Discourse in Journalism, Travel Writing,
                and Imperial Administration* (Durham, NC: Duke University Press).
Sugirtharajah, R.S.
    1993   'The Bible and its Asian Readers', *Biblical Interpretation: A Journal of
                Contemporary Approaches* 1(1): 54-66.
Wilson, Rob, and Wimal Dissanayake (eds.)
    1996   *Global/Local: Cultural Production and the Transnational Imaginary*
                (Durham, NC: Duke University Press).
Wongar, B.
    1983–86   *Walg* (New York: Dodd, Mead; Melbourne: Macmillan).
    1985–86   *Karan* (New York: Dodd, Mead; Melbourne: Macmillan).
    1987–88   *Gabo Djara* (New York: Dodd, Mead; Melbourne: Macmillan).

Biblical Criticism and Postcolonial Studies: Toward a Postcolonial Optic

FERNANDO F. SEGOVIA

In previous delineations of the paradigm of cultural studies in biblical criticism, I have sought to bring to the fore the constellation of elements that I regard as fundamental to this most recent and still emerging umbrella model of interpretation in the discipline (Segovia 1995a; 1995b; 1998). Two of these I see as particularly relevant for the present study. The first involves a view of all interpretation, all recreations of meaning from texts and all reconstructions of history, as dependent upon reading strategies and theoretical models, with a further view of all such strategies and models and the resultant recreations and reconstructions as constructs on the part of real readers. The second concerns a view of real or flesh-and-blood readers as variously positioned and engaged within their respective social locations, with a further view of all such contextualizations and perspectives as constructs on the part of real readers as well.

Needless to say, such views regarding the character of interpretation and the role of critics bear immediate consequences for the dynamics and mechanics of the paradigm as a whole.

First, the task of interpretation is viewed in terms of the application of different reading strategies and theoretical models—whether produced or borrowed—by different real readers in different ways, at different times, and with different results (different readings and interpretations) in the light of their different and highly complex situations and perspectives.

Second, a critical analysis of real readers and their readings (their representations of themselves as well as their representations of the ancient texts and the ancient world) becomes as important and necessary as a critical analysis of the ancient texts themselves (the remains of the ancient world).

Third, all recreations of meaning and all reconstructions of history are in the end regarded as representations of the past—recreations and reconstructions—on the part of readers who are themselves situated and interested to the core.

Finally, given its overriding focus on contextualization and perspective, social location and agenda, and thus on the political character of all compositions and texts, all readings and interpretations, all readers and interpreters, its mode of discourse may be described as profoundly ideological.

In this study I should like to proceed a step further in the definition and analysis of my own stance within the paradigm of cultural studies. In effect, I should like to lay the basic foundations and contours for what I have come to regard as a most appropriate, most enlightening, and most fruitful approach to biblical criticism, as I presently envision and practise the discipline. I have in mind the model of postcolonial studies, currently in vogue across a number of academic fields and disciplines.[1] This is a model that I find both hermeneutically rewarding and personally satisfying. On the one hand, I find that the model can shed precious, concomitant light on the various dimensions that I have posited as constitutive for my own vision and exercise of the

---

1.   There is no comprehensive—that is, cross-imperial and cross-colonial—study of postcolonial studies as such: no encompassing account of its origins, histories, and discourses across the various imperial/colonial experiences of Europe and the United States. There are, however, two very good readers. The first of these (Williams and Chrisman 1994) focuses on theory, as a listing of its chapters readily reveals: 'Theorizing Colonized Cultures and Anti-Colonial Resistance'; 'Theorizing the West'; 'Theorizing Gender'; 'Theorizing Post-Coloniality: Intellectuals and Institutions'; 'Theorizing Post-Coloniality: Discourse and Identity'; 'Reading from Theory'. The second (Ashcroft, Griffiths and Tiffin 1995) is organized according to themes, as again a listing of its chapters readily demonstrates: 'Issues and Debates'; 'Universality and Difference'; 'Representation and Resistance'; 'Postmodernism and Post-colonialism'; 'Nationalism'; 'Hybridity'; 'Ethnicity and Indigeneity'; 'Feminism and Post-colonialism'; 'Language'; 'The Body and Performance'; 'History'; 'Place'; 'Education'; 'Production and Consumption'. There are also two excellent studies of literary production in the postcolonial context, both with an emphasis on the anglophone world of the former British Empire (Ashcroft, Griffiths and Tiffin 1989; Boehmer 1995).

discipline. On the other hand, I find that the model speaks to me in a very direct way, not only as a contemporary biblical critic but also as a constructive theologian as well as a cultural critic.[2]

Option for a Postcolonial Optic

This is not the first time that I have had recourse to the language and concepts of postcolonial studies. Indeed, I have done so in the past both as a biblical critic and as a constructive theologian. I should like to recall such previous appeals as a point of departure for the present proposal regarding the adoption of a systematic and fully fledged postcolonial optic:[3]

First, from the point of view of my work in biblical criticism, I have described the development of biblical criticism from its beginning as an academic discipline in the early nineteenth century through to its present formation at the end of the twentieth

2. I can no longer describe myself solely as a biblical critic, despite my specific hiring, assignment and location in a Department of New Testament and Early Christianity within the context of the highly compartmentalized academic divisions of a Graduate Department of Religion based in a liberal Protestant Divinity School. At the very least, I must now describe myself as a constructive theologian as well, not only because I presently regard the traditional distinction between critic and theologian as having altogether collapsed but also because I see myself as engaged in the task of discoursing about the 'this-world' and the 'other-world' in the light of my own sociocultural and sociohistorical context in the diaspora, both as a child of the non-Western World and a child of a minority group within the West. Indeed, in the end, I would have to describe myself further as a cultural critic, insofar as I am also interested in these various dimensions of my social context quite aside from their socioreligious aspect. From this point of view, I am quite in agreement with the view that the call of the minority scholar is to engage in academic border crossings (JanMohamed and Lloyd 1990).

3. Within the model of postcolonial studies, terminology itself proves quite varied and thus problematic. Suffice it to say for now that by 'postcolonial' I mean ideological reflection on the discourse and practice of imperialism and colonialism from the vantage point of a situation where imperialism and colonialism have come—by and large though by no means altogether so—to a formal end but remain very much at work in practice, as neoimperialism and neocolonialism. Thus, the postcolonial optic is a field of vision forged in the wake of imperialism and colonialism but still very much conscious of their continuing, even if transformed, power.

century as a process of 'liberation' and 'decolonization' (Segovia 1995a: 8-9; 1995b: 2-7). To begin with, the development itself, I argued, involved the sequential emergence of four paradigms or umbrella models of interpretation: (1) the initial turn to and long reign of historical criticism, from early in the nineteenth century through to the third quarter of the twentieth century; (2) the rapid rise and steady consolidation of literary criticism and cultural or social criticism, beginning in the mid-1970s and continuing right through the present; (3) the recent irruption of cultural studies, beginning in the late 1980s and early 1990s. This development, I further argued, resulted in the present stage of competing modes of discourse within the discipline. Finally, such historical development and disciplinary dénouement I classified in terms of 'liberation' and 'decolonization' on two grounds.

First, with reference to a fundamental transformation in theoretical orientation and reading strategy. In the process, I pointed out, the long-dominant construct of the scientific reader—the universal, objective and impartial reader, fully decontextualized and non-ideological—yielded, slowly but surely, to the construct of the real reader—the local, perspectival and interested reader, always contextualized and ideological. Second, with reference to a fundamental transformation in the ranks of the discipline. In the process, I further pointed out, the male, clerical and European/Euro-American faces and concerns of the traditional practitioners of biblical criticism gave way, again gradually but steadily, to a variety of faces and concerns previously unknown to the discipline: at first, a large infusion of women from the West; subsequently, a growing presence of women and men from outside the West as well as from non-Western minorities in the West.

The end result of such transformations was not only enormous diversity in method and theory but also enormous diversity in faces and concerns within the discipline. This combined explosion of disciplinary perspectives and interpretive voices, I concluded, could and should be seen as a veritable process of liberation and decolonization: a movement away from the European and Euro-American voices and perspectives that had dominated biblical criticism for so long, toward a much more diversified and multicentered conception and exercise of the discipline. Biblical criticism, I observed, had become in the process but another example of a much more comprehensive process of liberation and decolonization at work in a number of different realms— from the political to the academic and, within the academy itself, across the entire disciplinary spectrum.

Second, from the point of view of my work in constructive theology, I have described the recent emergence of contextual theologies, both in the Two-Thirds World and among minorities of non-Western origin in the West, as an exercise in 'liberation' and 'decolonization' (Segovia 1992: 26-27). Thus, in setting out to formulate, as a distinctive expression within the rich matrix of US Hispanic American theology, a theology of the diaspora—a theology born and forged in exile, in displacement and relocation—I characterized it as both a 'liberation' and a 'postcolonial' theology (Segovia 1996a: 21-31; 1996b: 195-200).

Modern Christian theology, I argued, was a theology that emanated from the center, grounded as it was in Western civilization. As such, certain fundamental traits could be readily outlined: it was a systematic and universal theology, altogether reticent about its own social location and perspective; a theology of enlightenment and privilege, tacitly considered by nature superior to any theological production from outside the West—past, present or future; a theology of hegemony and mission, with the effective control and progressive civilization of the margins in mind. In contrast, I further argued, diaspora theology—like any other contextual theology—was a theology that emerged from the margins, in this case from the margins within the West itself. Consequently, certain fundamental traits could be readily delineated as well: it was a self-consciously local and constructive theology, quite forthcoming about its own social location and perspective; a theology of diversity and pluralism, highlighting the dignity and value of all matrices and voices, including its own; a theology of engagement and dialogue, committed to critical conversation with other theological voices from both margins and center alike.

The rapid and widespread rise of contextual theologies, such as US Hispanic American theology and my own theology of the diaspora, I concluded, could and should be seen as an undeniable process of 'liberation' and 'decolonization': a movement away from the long-standing control of theological production by European and Euro-American voices and perspectives, toward the

retrieval and revalorization of the full multiplicity of voices and
perspectives in the margins. As in the case of biblical criticism,
therefore, theological studies, I observed, had also become in the
process yet another example of the much more extensive process
of liberation and decolonization at work in the world and in the
academy.

Such past appeals on my part to the linguistic and conceptual
apparatus of postcolonial studies have been, though quite useful
and revealing to be sure, much too limited and unsystematic as
well. A more fundamental grounding and deployment of the
model is in order, therefore, and it is precisely this task that I
should like to undertake in the present study, with biblical criticism specifically in mind. I do so, once again, because of the rich
hermeneutical and personal dividends that I see as accruing from
an explicit and sustained use of the model.

On the one hand, as I indicated earlier, this is a model that
lends itself eminently to simultaneous application across the various dimensions that I see as central to my own conception and
exercise of the discipline: first, the level of texts—the analysis of
the texts of ancient Judaism and early Christianity; second, the
level of 'texts'—the analysis of readings and interpretations of
such texts in the modern, Western tradition; third, the level of
readers—the analysis of the modern and contemporary real readers of these texts and producers of the 'texts' both inside and outside the West. In other words, postcolonial studies can function
thereby as an excellent model for cross-cultural studies in the discipline, and in what follows I shall show how such is the case in
terms of these three major dimensions of the discipline.

On the other hand, as I also stated earlier, this is a model that
proves extremely appealing to me personally. The reason, I would
readily acknowledge, has to do with my own social location and
agenda: I come from the margins, from the world of the colonized; I reside in the center, in the world of the colonizers; and I
have devoted myself to the struggle for liberation and decolonization, for the sake of both the colonized and the colonizer. For me,
therefore, postcolonial studies not only comes from the heart, so
to speak, it also refreshes and invigorates the heart. A colonial
genealogy is in order.

The history of my own colonial mapping is quite complex. To

begin with, I am a child of the Caribbean Basin, one of the most highly colonized and contested sites of the globe, as both the almost total absence of indigenous peoples and the presence of anglophone, francophone and hispanophone populations readily attest. Here the project of imperialism and colonialism was so immensely successful and so radically effective that, in a relatively brief period of time, the original local populations had disappeared and the original local languages had been replaced. Indeed, in the Caribbean archipelago one has to go almost island by island to explain the imperial and colonial dynamics at work over the five centuries since the European 'discovery'. Then, with emigration and exile, a further distinguishing mark of the Caribbean Basin, I became a child of the diaspora, a part of the Hispanic American reality and experience in the United States, a context of internal colonialism not unlike that facing other groups from outside the West now residing in the West (Segovia 1992: 27-33; 1996a: 21-31).

In my own case, therefore, as a native of the island of Cuba and an exile-immigrant in the United States, such mapping entails four distinctive experiences of imperialism and colonialism: (1) the after-effects of possession by the Spanish Empire, from the very beginning of its landfall in 'the Americas' to the very demise of the empire itself—from the first voyage of Christopher Columbus to the Spanish–American War (1492–1898); (2) the continuing effects of occupation by the American Empire at the very apex of its period of manifest destiny (1898–1902) followed by the period of the republic (1902–59), a period of neocolonial dependency, marked by the watchful supervision of the United States, a number of military interventions by US forces, and a series of cruel and corrupt dictatorships—from the declaration of independence to the triumph of the Cuban Revolution; (3) the new effects from the implantation of a socialist-Leninist system of government at the very height of the Cold War, under the neocolonial aegis of the Soviet Empire (1959–89) followed by the continuation of such a system of government even after the total collapse of the imperial center (1989–present); (4) the situation of internal colonialism affecting by and large the Hispanic American population as a whole in the United States.

In the light of such a long and distinguished pedigree, it should come as no surprise that I regard and construct myself as carrying imperialism and colonialism in my flesh and in my soul, as a human subject and as a real, flesh-and-blood reader—and hence as a biblical critic, as a constructive theologian and as a cultural critic. For me, therefore, the reality of empire, of imperialism and colonialism, constitutes an omnipresent, inescapable and over-whelming reality. My option for a postcolonial optic should thus be obvious: it is a model that I find most helpful, most revealing and most liberating. In what follows, therefore, I proceed to unpack its particular importance and relevance for biblical criticism.

Postcolonial Studies and Biblical Criticism

Postcolonial studies is a model that takes the reality of empire, of imperialism and colonialism, as an omnipresent, inescapable and overwhelming reality in the world: the world of antiquity, the world of the Near East or of the Mediterranean Basin; the world of modernity, the world of Western hegemony and expansionism; and the world of today, of postmodernity, the world of postcolo-nialism on the part of the Two-Thirds World and of neocolonial-ism on the part of the West.

Postcolonial Studies and Ancient Texts
A first dimension of a postcolonial optic in biblical criticism involves an analysis of the texts of ancient Judaism and early Christianity that takes seriously into consideration their broader sociocultural contexts in the Near East and the Mediterranean Basin, respectively, in the light of an omnipresent, inescapable and overwhelming sociopolitical reality—the reality of empire, of imperialism and colonialism, as variously constituted and exer-cised during the long period in question. Some preliminary observations regarding this phenomenon of empire are in order.[4]

First, the reality of empire should be seen as a structural reality that is largely defined and practised in terms of a primary bino-mial: on the one hand, a political, economic and cultural

4.   For good, concise introductions to the phenomena of imperialism and colonialism in general, see Said (1990; 1993: 3-61 [Chapter 1: 'Over-lapping Territories, Intertwined Histories']; Deane 1994).

center—more often than not symbolized by a city; on the other hand, any number of margins politically, economically and culturally subordinated to the center. This grounding binomial entails and engenders, in turn, any number of secondary or subordinate binomials: civilized/uncivilized; advanced/primitive; cultured/barbarian; progressive/backward; developed/undeveloped –underdeveloped. Second, such a structural reality, despite the many and profound similarities in common, should not be seen as uniform in every imperial context across time and culture—say, for example, from the world of Assyria and Babylon, to the world of Greece and Rome, to the world of Western Europe and the United States—but as differentiated in constitution and deployment, though again with many and profound similarities in common. Third, this reality, I would argue, is of such reach and such power that it inevitably affects and colors, directly or indirectly, the entire artistic production of center and margins, of dominant and subaltern, including their respective literary productions.

From the point of view of ancient Judaism and its literature, it is necessary to speak not just of one empire but of a succession of empires involving, depending on the locality of the center in question, the Near East as well as the Mediterranean Basin: Assyria, Babylon, Persia, Greece, Rome. From the point of view of early Christianity and its literature, it is obviously the massive presence and might of the Roman Empire, master and lord of the entire Circum-Mediterranean, with its thoroughly accurate if enormously arrogant classification of the Mediterranean Sea as *mare nostrum*.

To begin with, therefore, the shadow of empire in the production of ancient texts is to be highlighted. A number of key questions come to the fore as a result: How do the margins look at the 'world'—a world dominated by the reality of empire—and fashion life in such a world? How does the center regard and treat the margins in the light of its own view of the 'world' and life in that world? What images and representations of the other-world arise from either side? How is history conceived and constructed by both sides? How is 'the other' regarded and represented? What conceptions of oppression and justice are to be found? From the

perspective of postcolonial studies, such questions—questions of
culture, ideology, and power—emerge as crucial.

Postcolonial Studies and Modern Readings
A second dimension of the proposed postcolonial optic in biblical
criticism involves an analysis of the readings and interpretations
of the texts of Jewish and Christian antiquity that takes seriously
into account their broader sociocultural context in the West,
whether by way of Europe or of North America, in the light of the
same omnipresent, inescapable, and overwhelming sociopolitical
reality that surrounded the production of the texts of ancient
Judaism and early Christianity—the reality of empire, of imperialism and colonialism, now with regard to the Western imperial
tradition of the last five hundred years.

First, the imperial tradition of the West may be approached in
terms of three different phases and periods:[5] (1) early imperialism, with reference to the initial, mercantile phase of European
imperialism—from the fifteenth century through most of the
nineteenth century, from the monarchical states of Portugal and
Spain to the early modern states of England, France and the
Netherlands, among others; (2) high imperialism, involving
monopoly capitalism with its integration of industrial and finance
capital in the major capitalist nation-states—from the end of the
nineteenth century through to the middle of the twentieth century, with England as prime example; and (3) late imperialism,
with reference to both the end of formal colonialism and the continued impact and power of imperial culture in the world—from
mid-century to the present, with the United States as its prime
example.

Second, this tradition of Western empire-building was accompanied by a very prominent socioreligious dimension as well.
Thus, the Western missionary movement may be divided into two
major waves and periods, represented by the highly symbolic
dates of 1492 and 1792.[6] The first date stands, of course, for the

5.   I find myself in agreement with the caution offered for postcolonial
studies in general by Michael Sprinker (1996: 1-10), who insists on the need
to offer and follow a historical periodization of the different types of imperialism at work in the West over this period of five centuries.
6.   I follow here the thesis of Andrew Walls (1995).

first European landfall in the 'New World'. This first stage of the missions (1492–1792) is primarily Catholic in orientation, involves the massive evangelization of the Americas, and finds itself near exhaustion by the end of the eighteenth century. The second date, not as well known, recalls two different though related events: first, with regard to Asia (India), the publication of William Carey's *Enquiry into the obligation of Christians to use means for the propagation of the Gospel among the heathens* and concomitant formation of his missionary society; second, with regard to Africa (Sierra Leone), the establishment of the first church in tropical Africa in modern times (interestingly enough, by people of African birth or descent from North America). This second stage (1792–present) is at first primarily Protestant in nature, concerns the massive evangelization of Africa, Asia and remaining areas of the Americas, and remains quite vigorous today. Over the last five centuries, therefore, the different phases of European imperialism and colonialism brought with them, wherever they turned, their respective religious beliefs and practices, whether Catholic or Protestant.

Third, a comparison of this twofold division of the missionary movement of the West with the previous threefold division of Western imperialism proves instructive. On the one hand, the first missionary wave of the fifteenth through the eighteenth centuries coincides with the first imperialist phase—the mercantile stage of early imperialism; on the other hand, the second missionary wave of the nineteenth and twentieth centuries coincides with the transition from the first to the second imperialist phase in the nineteenth century and its full bloom at the end of the nineteenth century and the beginning of the twentieth—the monopoly capitalist stage of high imperialism.

As such, the structural binomial reality of empire should be seen as involving a strong socioreligious component as well. The political, economic and cultural center also functions as a religious center; that is to say, the practices and beliefs of the center are invariably grounded on, sanctioned and accompanied by a set of religious beliefs and practices. Consequently, the primary binomial of center and margins entails and engenders a further binomial in this sphere as well: believers/unbelievers–pagans, which in turn gives rise to a number of other secondary and

subordinate binomials, such as godly/ungodly (worshippers of
the true God/worshippers of false gods) and religious/idol-
atrous–superstitious. As a result, the margins politically, economically and culturally subordinated to the center must be brought
into religious submission as well: their religious beliefs must be
corrected and uplifted; their gods attacked and destroyed; their
practices ridiculed and replaced.

Finally, such a reality, I would argue once again, further colors
and affects, directly or indirectly, the entire artistic production of
both center and margins, the dominant and the subaltern, including their respective literary productions.

From the point of view of biblical criticism, therefore, it is clear
that the academic study of the texts of ancient Judaism and early
Christianity, given the formation and consolidation of the discipline in the course of the nineteenth century, parallels the second
major wave of the Western missionary movement as well as the
transition period to the second, high phase of Western imperialism and colonialism: first, as Europe turns to Africa and Asia, in a
renewed and frantic scramble for territories and possessions;
second, as the United States turns West and beyond, with its eyes
increasingly set on the islands of the Caribbean, the heart of
Mexico and territories in the Pacific.

Consequently, the shadow of empire in the production of
modern readings of the ancient texts should also be underlined.
In the process, certain crucial questions again come to the surface, not unlike those raised earlier but now from a different
angle: How do such readings and interpretations, coming from
the metropolitan centers of the West as they do, address and present such issues in the ancient texts as empire and margins,
oppression and justice; the world and life in the world as well as
the other-world and its inhabitants; history and 'the other', mission and conversion, followers and outsiders; salvation, election
and holiness? Once again, from the point of view of postcolonial
studies, questions such as these—questions of culture, ideology
and power—prove all-important.

Postcolonial Studies and Readers
For this third dimension of the proposed postcolonial optic in
biblical criticism, I would argue once more for an analysis of the

readers of the texts of ancient Judaism and early Christianity that takes seriously into consideration their broader sociocultural contexts in the global sphere, whether in the West or outside the West, in the light of the same omnipresent, inescapable and overwhelming sociopolitical reality that engulfed the texts of Jewish and Christian antiquity as well as the readings and interpretations of such texts in the West—the reality of empire, of imperialism and colonialism, now in terms of not only the Western imperial tradition of the last five centuries but also the reaction against such a tradition from outside the West within the context of the postcolonial yet neocolonial world of the last half-century. Some preliminary observations are once again in order.

First, despite what I have described as its omnipresent, inescapable and overwhelming character, the structural binomial reality of imperialism and colonialism is never imposed or accepted in an atmosphere of absolute and undisturbed passivity. Always in the wake of the fundamental binomial of center/margins, and ultimately deconstructing it as well, in principle if not in praxis, lies the inverted binomial of resistance/fear. I say 'inverted' because this is the one binomial opposition where the margins actually take the initiative, while the center is forced into a reactive position.

In effect, there is always—sooner or later, major or minor, explicit or implicit—resistance to the center on the part of the politically, economically, culturally and religiously subordinated margins, even when such resistance brings about, as it inevitably does, further measures of control on the part of the center, designed to instil fear into the minds and hearts of the margins. Such measures, to be sure, only serve to contribute to a further deconstruction of the binomial reality, as the civilized, advanced, cultured, progressive, developed and believing center turns increasingly to measures of an uncivilized, primitive, barbarian, backward, undeveloped and unbelieving order against the marginal groups. At some point, such resistance on the part of the margins may come to a climax, and this climax may involve in turn a variety of gradations: open challenge and defiance; widespread rebellion and anomie; actual overthrow and reorientation.

Second, I would argue that such resistance is precisely what has occurred in the discipline in the last quarter of the century, as more and more outsiders have joined its ranks. Such outsiders can be classified according to two groupings: women from the West; men and women from outside the West as well as from ethnic and racial minorities in the West. In both cases, a similar pattern of resistance can be observed: early stirrings in the 1970s—what could be called a situation of open challenge and defiance; maturation and solidification through the 1980s—a clear situation of widespread rebellion and anomie; sharpened sophistication in the 1990s—what could be compared to a situation of actual overthrow and reorientation.

Third, it should not go unobserved that such disciplinary changes take place not long after the commencement of the third major phase of Western imperialism and colonialism, marked by the end of formal colonialism, with wars of independence and the loss of colonies everywhere—the age of the postcolonial, and the continued impact of imperial culture everywhere—the age of the neocolonial. More specifically, such developments, one should recall, come soon after the crisis experienced by the West, both in Europe and North America, during the late 1960s and the early 1970s. Quite clearly, the upheaval in the world at large ultimately affects the discipline as well.

Finally, such a reality, I would argue yet again, does affect and color as well, directly or indirectly, the entire artistic production of center and margins, dominant and subaltern, including their respective literary productions.

From the point of view of biblical critics, then, it now becomes necessary to distinguish between two general groupings. On the one hand, those readers associated with the long imperial tradition of the West, especially from the time of transition to high imperialism to the present phase of neocolonialism within late imperialism—still the vast majority of critics; on the other hand, those critics associated with the colonies of the Western empires, what has come to be known as the 'Two-Thirds World', now raising their voices for the first time during the present phase of postcolonialism within late imperialism—a growing minority of critics.

Therefore, the shadow of empire in the lives of modern as well as contemporary readers must, yet again, be highlighted in biblical criticism. In so doing, a number of crucial questions come to the fore, similar to those outlined before but formulated from yet another angle of approach: how do traditional (male) critics, from the metropolitan centers of the West, stand—and construct them-'selves'—with regard to the relationship between empire and margins, the West and the rest, Christendom and outsiders; mission and conversion, oppression and justice, history and the other; salvation, election and holiness; the this-world and life in the world as well as the other-world? What is the position of Western women in this regard, in their role as previous outsiders from the West itself? How do men and women from outside the West as well as from ethnic and racial minorities in the West respond to such issues? Such questions—questions of culture, ideology and power—emerge as all-important, from the point of view of postcolonial studies.

Concluding Comments

From the point of view of cultural studies, that paradigm within which I presently situate myself in the discipline, the model of postcolonial studies should be seen as one major line of approach, alongside others. Such a line of approach, furthermore, should also be seen as quite broad and quite rich—multidimensional, multicentered, multilingual. Not only is its theoretical apparatus immense and its range of reading strategies phenomenal, as reflected in the exploding corpus of critical literature, but also its scope and its reach prove to be radically global as well, drawing as it does on the discourses and practices of imperialism and colonialism across cultures and historical periods.

In the introduction I remarked that, as a model within cultural studies—an intermediate model within an umbrella model, as it were—postcolonial studies proves most appropriate, most enlightening, and most fruitful. The reasons should now be evident.

First, the model is not only thoroughly self-conscious of itself as a construct, dependent upon certain theoretical claims and reading strategies, but also calls for self-consciousness on the part of its would-be practitioners as constructs, dependent upon certain representations of themselves, of their own social locations and agendas, as real readers. Both with regard to interpretation and

interpreters, therefore, the model presupposes and demands a
specific optic with clear implications for both the representation
of the past and the representation of the present.

Second, the model can address at one and the same time the
various interrelated and interdependent dimensions of criticism:
the analysis of texts—the world of antiquity; the analysis of
'texts'—the world of modernity; the analysis of readers of texts
and producers of 'texts'—the world of postmodernity.

Finally, the model is profoundly ideological, for it looks upon
the political experience of imperialism and colonialism as central
to the task of criticism at all levels of inquiry.

In the end, however, as a model within cultural studies, postcolonial studies has no choice but to see itself and represent itself
as *unus inter pares*; otherwise, it could easily turn into an imperial
discourse of its own. It is an optic, not the optic, in full engagement and dialogue with a host of other models and other optics.
Yet, even as one among equals, it proves most incisive and most
telling, for it reminds us all, the children of the colonized and the
children of the colonizer, that the discipline of biblical criticism
as we know it and have known it must be seen and analyzed, like
all other discourses of modernity, against the much broader
geopolitical context of Western imperialism and colonialism. In
so doing, furthermore, the goal is not merely one of analysis and
description but rather one of transformation: the struggle for
'liberation' and 'decolonization'.

BIBLIOGRAPHY

Ashcroft, Bill, Gareth Griffiths and Helen Tiffin (eds.)
    1989   *The Empire Writes Back: Theory and Practice in Post-colonial Literatures*
                (London: Routledge & Kegan Paul).
    1995   *The Post-Colonial Studies Reader* (London: Routledge & Kegan Paul).
Boehmer, Elleke
    1995   *Colonial and Postcolonial Literature: Migrant Metaphors* (Oxford:
                Oxford University Press).
Deane, Seamus
    1994   'Imperialism and Nationalism', in Frank L. Lentricchia and Thomas
                McLaughlin (eds.), *Critical Terms for Literary Study* (Chicago: Univer-
                sity of Chicago Press, 2nd enl. edn): 354-68.

JanMohamed, Abdul R., and David Lloyd (eds.)

    1990   'Introduction: Toward a Theory of Minority Discourse: What Is to Be Done?', in *The Nature and Context of Minority Discourse* (Oxford: Oxford University Press): 1-16.

Said, Edward

    1990   'Yeats and Decolonization', in Seamus Deane (ed.), *Nationalism, Colonialism, and Literature* (Minneapolis: University of Minnesota Press): 69-95.

    1993   *Culture and Imperialism* (New York: Alfred A. Knopf).

Segovia, Fernando F.

    1992   'Two Places and No Place on Which to Stand: Mixture and Otherness in Hispanic American Theology', in Fernando F. Segovia (ed.), *Hispanic Americans in Theology and the Church* (Special issue of *Listening: Journal of Religion and Culture* 27): 26-40.

    1995a   ' "And They Began to Speak in Other Tongues": Competing Modes of Discourse in Contemporary Biblical Criticism', in F.F. Segovia and M.A. Tolbert (eds.), *Reading from This Place. I. Social Location and Biblical Interpretation in the United States* (Minneapolis: Fortress Press): 1-32.

    1995b   'Cultural Studies and Contemporary Biblical Criticism: Ideological Criticism as Mode of Discourse', in F.F. Segovia and M.A. Tolbert (eds.), *Reading from This Place. II. Social Location and Biblical Interpretation in Global Perspective* (Minneapolis: Fortress Press): 1-17.

    1996a   'Aliens in the Promised Land: The Manifest Destiny of U.S. Hispanic American Theology', in Ada María Isasi-Díaz and Fernando F. Segovia (eds.), *Hispanic/Latino Theology: Challenge and Promise* (Minneapolis: Fortress Press): 15-42.

    1996b   'In the World but Not of It: Exile as a Locus for a Theology of the Diaspora', in Ada María Isasi-Díaz and Fernando F. Segovia (eds.), *Hispanic/Latino Theology: Challenge and Promise* (Minneapolis: Fortress Press): 195-217.

    1998   'Pedagogical Discourse and Practices in Cultural Studies: Toward a Contextual Pedagogy of the Bible', in F.F. Segovia and M.A. Tolbert (eds.), *Teaching the Bible: The Discourses and Politics of Biblical Pedagogy* (Maryknoll: Orbis Books, forthcoming).

Sprinker, Michael

    1996   'Introduction', in R. de la Campa, E. Ann Kaplan and M. Sprinker (eds.), *Late Imperial Culture* (London: Verso): 1-10.

Walls, Andrew

    1995   'Christianity in the Non-Western World: A Study in the Serial Nature of Christian Expansion', *Studies in World Christianity* 1: 1-25.

Williams P., and L. Chrisman (eds.)

    1994   *Colonial Discourse and Post-Colonial Theory: A Reader* (New York: Columbia University Press).

The Danger of Ignoring One's Own Cultural Bias in Interpreting the Text

RANDALL C. BAILEY

Black biblical interpretation in Africa began in biblical times, since the bible was written in north east Africa (= Ancient Israel). Black biblical interpretation in the Caribbean, the UK, US and other parts of the African diaspora has been going on since we first heard the gospel (Lincoln and Mamiya 1990; Raboteau 1978, 1995; Servett 1985; and Wilmore 1983). This interpretation varies widely. As James Evans (1992) notes, on the one hand, there has been the strand which centered on the Exodus motif and the liberation from Egypt of the Hebrew children, while on the other, there has been the strand which has highlighted the presence of African people in the text. Bishop Henry McNeil Turner argued an Afrocentric interpretation of the deity in his essay entitled, 'God Is a Negro' (Wilmore 1983: 257 n. 4). There is a long tradition of interpreting Ps. 68.31

> Let bronze be brought from Egypt;
>   let Ethiopia hasten to stretch out its hands

as a prophecy of the rise and return of African people to the grand status of ancient days (Raboteau 1995: 37-56). Harriet Tubman was termed 'Moses', a designation which underscored a non-patriarchal appropriation of the tradition. Marcus Garvey bespoke the return to Africa as a new Exodus. John Holder in Barbados has called for a new Jubilee, while Bishop Wilfred Wood (1994) a black Anglican bishop in the UK, enjoins us to *Keep the Faith, Baby*.

In this article I would like to explore and critique various modes of Afrocentric biblical interpretation, as they have functioned throughout the centuries. In particular I shall concentrate on my own traditions from my ancestors and contemporaries in the US, with attempts to apply these to the current context of blacks in the various locations of the African diaspora and on the continent. In so doing I shall begin my examination with the use of biblical themes and images in the spirituals.

Within postcolonial models of analysis this literature conforms to the race-based category (Ashcroft *et al.* 1989). To some extent there is a hybridization in the approaches which will be discussed here, as we have been influenced by our varied contexts, theological and ideological commitments, and methods of interpretation. In no sense is there any one construct of black biblical interpretation, but, as will be argued here, there is a wide variety of approaches and agendas carried out under this rubric.

I

The spirituals attest to the incorporation of biblical themes in intriguing ways of interpretation (Copher 1986a). As my colleague, Melva Costen, writes, 'Properly understood, Spirituals… are analogous to theological documents carefully and thoughtfully presented in simple and often symbolic language…' (1993: 95). Similarly, it has been argued that the spirituals contain coded language which bespeaks political resistance to oppression (Lovell 1972; Fisher 1990). Our claim to the Exodus story is noted in the words to 'Go Down Moses'. As the lyric goes:

> When Israel was in Egypt land,
> > Let my people go.
> Oppressed so hard they could not stand,
> > Let my people go.
> Go down, Moses, way down to Egypt land.
> > Tell ole Pharaoh to let my people go.

This song bespoke our desires for freedom and liberation from slavery, with the hope of finding, or as Theophilus Smith (1994) would argue, conjuring up, our own Moses to go to Pharaoh.

Our hopes for liberation and reconciliation are heard in the spiritual 'Let Us Break Bread Together on our Knees'. This song expressed the desire to engage in the Eucharist in community with all people, both those who were part of our group and those who were excluding us (cf. Owens 1971: 109-14). Let us do it together. As the lyric states, 'Let us break bread/drink wine/ praise God together on our knees'. In the face of a history of seg- regated religious practices, this song spoke of a hope for reconcil- iation. One vividly remembers the dramatic expulsion of Richard Allen and Absalom Jones from St George Methodist Episcopal Church in Philadelphia, which led to the establishment of the African Methodist Episcopal Church and the first black Episcopal Church. One also thinks of the establishment of mission churches in various denominations for the blacks, while in the same city the missionaries started all-white congregations for their own families to hold worship. One also thinks of the reaction of the white churches in England to the migration of Caribbean peoples there, a reaction of exclusion and rejection of these people of the same faith but of a different race. One thinks of the years of racist interpretation of the curse of Cain and the so-called 'curse of Ham' in the US and the theological justification for apartheid using the Tower of Babel narratives.

Remarkably, in the face of such dehumanization, instead of telling these people to take their religion and shove it, there was the call for coming together to eat bread, drink wine and praise God in the Eucharist, to share the broken body and spilt blood of Christ together. As Dwight Hopkins has argued, 'black folks rejected these scurrilous and heretical faith claims [of non-human status ascribed them]. Though physically bound, slaves neverthe- less directly encountered the biblical God in their own theological creativity' (1993: 22).

At the same time there was in the spiritual 'Let Us Break Bread Together' a recognition and celebration of our African roots as they sang 'with my face to the rising sun'. This implies the singing facing Africa, to the east, from whence comes the sun in the morning.

By the same token the refrain of this particular spiritual resists the *hybris*, pride, of those who are willing and desirous of being inclusive. This is seen in the words 'O, Lord, have mercy on me'. I may desire inclusivity, in response to a context which is exclusive, but I also realize my need for forgiveness in other areas. In essence the whole meaning of the song is, let us worship together, but do not require that I give up my own African culture, while I also understand my own need for forgiveness. Thus, this spiritual encompasses several theological and biblical motifs and metaphors.

This sense of reconciliation between oppressed and oppressor is a minority report in the spirituals, however. As Earl notes, 'Lyricized conversion language gave slaves a radical sense of being free to dialogue together in the face of their slave masters' oppressive monological structure of communication. It afforded them, indirectly, a creative way to critique the oppressive nature of their masters' monologues' (1993: 71).

The theme of divine retributive justice for the oppressor, on the other hand, sounds in other spirituals. For instance, in the spiritual 'All God's Chillun Got Shoes', after making the claim to having those resources which are presently illegitimately denied to us here on earth,

> I got shoes, you got shoes,
>   all God's Chillun got shoes,

and after affirming the claim to receiving those resources at a future time

> When I get to Heb'n
> I'm gonna put on my shoes

there is the disclaimer that

> Everyone talkin' 'bout Heb'n isn't goin' der!

I can imagine my fore-parents standing outside the white folks' churches with the horses and carriages, not allowed into the church of their slave-owning bosses, singing this song, relishing the ultimate payback to their oppressors. 'You may be inside the church praying to your God, but in the end you ain't goin' to Heb'n, 'cause of de way you treatin' us' (cf. Thurman 1975: 47-55). This is a faith affirmation in the spirit of 'Not everyone who says to me, "Lord, Lord", will enter the kingdom of heaven' (Mt. 7.21).

The spiritual 'O Mary Don't You Weep' demonstrates an interesting and contrastive aspect of US Afrocentric biblical interpretation. The refrain is:

> O, Mary don't you weep,
> O, Martha don't you moan.
> 'Cause Pharaoh's army got drownded.

On the one hand, there is agreement or assent to the interrelation of Hebrew Scripture and the New Testament theme, as made by the broader Christian community, in the reference to Mary and Martha in the Gospel of John and the reference to Pharaoh in the book of Exodus. This is similar to the spiritual

> We Are Climbing Jacob's Ladder,
> Soldiers of the Cross,

where there is a joining of the patriarchal narratives of Genesis and the passion narratives of the Gospels.

In 'O, Mary, O, Martha', on the other hand, there is the connection of what appear to be disparate images. What do Mary and Martha have to do with Pharaoh? The opening verses refer to Mary and Martha at the tomb of Lazarus crying over his death and Jesus not coming soon enough to prevent it, as recorded in John 11. What is interesting in this spiritual is that, while Jn 11.25 gives as the reason for them to stop crying namely that Jesus is the 'resurrection and the life' (cf. Brown 1970; Bultmann 1971; and Morris 1971), the spiritual, instead, appeals to the drowning of Pharaoh's army as the reason not to cry. This combination of themes has been explained as a claim that the God of the Exodus is the God of the Resurrection, which keeps the song closer to the text of John 11 and defuses the violent image of the drowning army.

It appears that the reference to the drowning in the sea in Exodus 14 (cf. Durham 1987: 194-98), however, is to the destruction of the oppressor (Owens 1971: 56) rather than to the liberation of the people. Thus, the song is telling Mary and Martha not to weep over the death of their loved one, because God is the one who will kill the oppressor. To those Africans enslaved in the US who saw their men killed and their women raped in situations where it appeared that God was not 'showing up' to protect them and keep them alive, as in John 11; in the final analysis, not the resurrection, but the drowning of the oppressor in the sea was the hope for the future.[1] Clearly, the ethic of praying for the enemy

---

1.   This could be an example of the claim that every generation must see and claim the Gospel in its own existential situation (cf. Käsemann 1969: 150-52). If so, this would be a break with the original intention of the Gospel which, as currently argued to be, 'In the concrete situation of the Johannine

in Mt. 5.43 had taken on a new meaning to my ancestors.

Another aspect of this conflation, or joining together in one literary unit, of Hebrew Scripture and New Testament tradition is seen in the spiritual 'They Crucified my Savior, and He Never Said a Mumbling Word'. This spiritual refers to the passion narrative. That group of stories has in it what we now call 'The Seven Last Words', statements which Jesus is reported to have made from the cross. The spiritual, however, states, 'and he never said a mumbling word'. It appears that my fore-parents did not like the Seven Last Words tradition. Instead, it appears that they opted for the 'suffering servant' in Isaiah 42 and 53 (cf. Watts 1987), where the servant did not verbally protest. As Isa. 42.2 states,

> He will not cry or lift up his voice
> or make it heard in the street.

And Isa. 53.7 states,

> He was oppressed, and he was afflicted
> yet he did not open his mouth.

This understanding of the spiritual suggests that they were not bound by the biblical text; rather they felt they could critique it and modify it as they expressed their religious experiences. Significantly, the modification of the motif is in line with African martyrdom traditions, where the martyr does not dignify the oppressive lynching by giving human verbal expression. This is seen not only in the refusal of Nat Turner to speak at his own murder, but in other such tales of African martyrdom. In this way we note that, as with other forms of liberative exegesis, the exegete openly begins with experience as a category. As Zora Neal Hurston, the famed black writer of the Harlem Renaissance stated, 'Even the Bible was made over to suit our vivid imagination' (1990: 3).

A major difference between Afrocentric biblical interpretation and Eurocentric interpretation was the sense of the immanence of the supernatural and miraculous. The spiritual 'My Lord Delivered Daniel, Why Not Me' bespeaks the expectation that just as

community, this means that, forcibly cut off from their religious heritage, they have concentrated that heritage, its observances and its hopes, entirely in the figure of Jesus' (Rensberger 1988: 120).

God intervened in history in the biblical narrative and rescued
oppressed people, who were faced with life-threatening situations,
such as Daniel in the lion's den, where God protects him, so God
will replicate that action for us (Cone 1975; Townes 1993). In a
sense this is the same understanding as 'Go Down Moses'. The
added dimension of this song is the open expectation that God
will intervene in miraculous ways. This appropriation is antitheti-
cal to rationalism's hold on theological speculation in Eurocentric
theological discourse, as argued by Robert Hood in his book, *Must
God Remain Greek?* He argues that Eurocentric theology became
captive to Aristotelian and, in places, Platonic thought and was
locked into these formulations of reality, which opened certain
theological notions, but closed others.

The political nature of religion is also seen in the message of
the spirituals. In 'O, Freedom Over Me' the chorus goes,

> And before I'd be a slave,
> I'll be buried in my grave,
> And go home to my Lord, and be free!

This makes the claim of the centrality of liberation to the black
religious experience. As the song says, death, even suicide, is a
preferable theological option to oppression. 'People Get Ready,
There's a Train a Comin'' was an announcement on the plantation that the Underground Railroad was in operation that night.
Similarly, 'Steal Away to Jesus' bespoke the sanction to run away
from slavery. By the same token, 'There's No Hiding Place' would
be sung by Africans in the fields letting those who were on the run
know that the overseers were searching for them on that plantation and not to stop there.

In other words, the spirituals became a way of political communication among the initiated, which would be safe in the presence
of the oppressor, in the same way that apocalyptic literature found
in the bible was coded to enable the Judeans, oppressed by the
Greeks and Romans, and the members of the early church,
oppressed by the Romans, to resist the oppression and to struggle
for their freedom. At the same time, this side of the spirituals
attests to a long tradition within the black religious experience
of insurgency and subversion of the existing social order. We
must also remember, however, the other notion of reconciliation
with the oppressor, as noted above in other spirituals. Thus, the

spirituals give us a glimpse of the history and freedom of black Christian interpretation.

It must be noted that this form of appropriation of biblical imagery and symbols, and of reforming them by means of fusing different narratives, was not restricted to the spirituals. Listen to the words of David Walker's *Appeal to the Coloured Citizens of the World*, issued in 1829.

> Though our cruel oppressors and murderers, may (if possible) treat us more cruel, as Pharaoh did the Children of Israel, yet the God of the Ethiopians, has been pleased to hear our moans in consequence of oppression, and the day of our redemption from abject wretchedness draweth near, when we shall be enabled, in the most extended senses of the word, to stretch forth our hand to the Lord our God (1965: xiv).

In this statement from Walker, we see the references both to the liberation narratives of Exodus 1–14, and also to Ps. 68.28-31, where Egypt and Ethiopia are depicted as bringing gifts to the God of Israel in a universalist proclamation, where Ethiopia stretches forth her hands. There is also appeal to the Apocalypse with the references to the Day of Judgment, when the oppressor will be punished.

In this regard we see usage of biblical texts in ways which promote the liberation of black people living under genocidal conditions. The central tenet of interpretation was liberation and the giving of life. That which was supportive of this claim to life was to be embraced. That which was not, was to be reformed, reshaped, re-presented, or rejected. This occurred in the religious music, the spirituals, as well as in the political discourse.

This freedom of interpretation is best illustrated by Howard Thurman, who tells us of his reading the bible to his grandmother. She would not let him read to her, however, from the writings of Paul, except for the love hymn in 1 Corinthians 13, because of the use of the injunction, 'slaves be obedient to your masters', and the way it was used on the plantation (1981: 30-31). This incident shows the awareness of the political nature and use of the text and our right to reject it outright. As will be shown below, however, while many of us black biblical scholars quote this story, very few of us still openly exercise this option on biblical texts other than the slave injunctions. It seems we may have

forgotten our legacy or we may not have taken seriously enough
our own traditions.

II

As Vincent Wimbush (1991) argues, we in the US have adopted
the whole language world of the bible as a means of explaining
reality. We justify our claims to be free from the story of the
Exodus. We stake our claims on our humanity, that we were made
in the image of God, on Gen. 1.26-27. On the one hand, this text
was used to give strong force to the claim. On the other hand, it
was used for its rhetorically persuasive force with the ones who
professed belief in the bible. As C. Eric Lincoln claimed, there was
a deep-seated notion that adoption of the religion of the oppressor would lead to liberative results both in terms of manumission
and later integration (1978).

Incorporation, or adoption, to use Wimbush's term, of the language world of the bible also entailed, in part, the adoption of the
interpretation and symbols of the oppressor. Thus, there was a
negative psychological aspect of the phenomenon digested by us,
which we need to examine more fully.

A major starting point is a 'white Jesus'. It should be noted that
the depiction of biblical characters as Europeans, though begun
in Byzantium and further developed during Europe's Middle
Ages, became most prominent in the fifteenth and later centuries.
Most of the people in Europe were illiterate. Instead of teaching
them to read, artists were commissioned by the church to paint
pictures depicting bible stories so that the people could look at
the pictures and remember the story. As a tool of evangelism they
painted the characters and scenery to look like the locality where
the artist lived. Thus, Italians saw bible stories depicted as though
the people looked Italian and the scenery looked like Italian
villages. So also those in Germany, the Netherlands, and the like.
In this way, the Last Supper looks like a Roman feast (cf. Ferguson
1958; Piper 1991; Adams and Apostolos-Capadona 1987). These
depictions were done as a strategy of evangelism in order to help
the people better identify with the picture and the story. The fact
that these pictures were a historical distortion did not matter to
the artists, the church, or the people.

A major problem with these pictures, however, is that we have taken these pictures to be historical realities. We accepted the blond-haired, blue-eyed Jesus as an accurate depiction. We accepted Michelangelo's David and Moses as accurate depictions. As white supremacy grew and developed under the guise of scientific and rational objectivity, we accepted these pictures as accurate and even as desirable. As theories of the superiority of whites to other people in the name of 'civilization' grew, so did our self-hatred and adoption of the symbols (DuBois 1965; Fanon 1963).

When distorted, white supremacist theories developed, such as the concept of Hellenization (Hengel 1974), we bought them wholesale. The Greeks were not only good conquerors, they were also masterful imitators and incorporators of the culture of other people. This syncretism of Greco-Roman culture with indigenous culture was termed 'Hellenism'. To name the syncretism after only one of the parties, however, is a supremacist or hegemonic ploy. Thus, the term 'Hellenism' is a white supremacist term to make us think that the Greeks had more influence on the ancient world than they did. One could look at apologists like Josephus, to note that he tried to elevate the Greco-Roman esteem of Judaism by making claims such as the one that Abraham taught the Egyptians mathematics and astrology when he and Sarah went to Egypt (*Ant.* 1.8.2). Such claims give us evidence of how much of ancient Egyptian culture was valued by the northern invaders.[2] As Bernal (1987) and Van Sertimer (1976) have argued, the route of influence in the ancient world went from the south to the north, and not vice versa, as most historians of the ancient world have argued.

Another white supremacist term central to biblical interpretation is the term 'white' itself. In Exodus 4, when Moses balks at going to the children of Israel, God gives him some magic tricks to do. One of them is to stick his hand in his shirt. When he pulls it out, it has turned 'leprous, as white as snow'. He is then told to put it back in and it returns to its original state. Clearly, being white is no blessing in this passage. Similarly, in Numbers 12, as a punishment for challenging Moses' status on the basis of his

2.   In fact, this would be a very helpful way of reading Josephus and would make for an excellent dissertation, as well as documenting the contribution of an indigenous culture to the syncretism called 'Hellenism'.

marriage to a Cushite woman and talking to God, Miriam is turned 'leprous, as white as snow'.

Eurocentric interpretation has ignored such Hebrew Scripture understanding of 'white' as a curse, and even has mistranslated Isa. 1.18,

> Come let us reason together, says the LORD,
> though your sins are as scarlet,
>> they shall be made white as snow.

The Hebrew term translated as 'though' is *'im*. In all other instances of the term, it is translated as 'if'. In this instance, replacing 'if' with 'though' turns the statement from a judgment speech to a salvation oracle, with white as snow being changed from a curse to a blessing (Bailey 1996).

Clearly the task of translation is not an objective activity. Rather it is a heavily laced ideological, theological and philosophical activity (Spivak 1993; Bailey and Pippin 1996). That which is conceivable within the ideology of the translator is what gets translated. For example, Song 1.5

> I am black [conjunction] beautiful

uses the Hebrew conjunction *waw*, which can be translated either 'and' or 'but'. Thus, the exegetical translation task is, does the text read 'I am black and beautiful', as the NRSV translates it, or, 'I am black but comely', as other English translations read? The poetry of the passage shows that the person is speaking positively of herself, thus, it should be translated 'and'. The Greek translation recognized this and translated the conjunction with *kai*, 'and'. Jerome, when he translated the text into Latin, could not conceive of someone being 'black and beautiful'. Thus he translated the conjunction as *sed*, 'but'. The King James translators agreed with Jerome and translated it as 'dark but comely', where they could not even admit the possibility of one being 'black'.[3]

As noted earlier, one of the problems with this adoption of the language and symbol world of the bible and biblical interpretation is that we have in the latter instance incorporated white supremacy. For example, how long would it take for us to count

---

3. I am intrigued with the black church's being so wed to the KJV, given its status as being the most racist of all English translations.

the number of black churches in the US, Caribbean, UK and Africa with pictures of a white Jesus in them? As Gen. 15.5 states, 'Look toward heaven and count the stars, if you are able to count them.' We have all grown up with these icons to white supremacy emblazoned in our psyches.

Go into almost any black Protestant church in the US on communion Sunday and you will most probably see the table draped in white, the choirs and lay leaders dressed in white, the clergy robed in white, and possibly also the furniture draped in white. All of this white signals to the worshipper that something pure is about to happen. This idolatry of whiteness is carried in the liturgical colors of white for Christmas and Eastertide, dark purple for Advent and Lent, and black for Good Friday. Even in a postcolonial context this symbolic world is still flourishing.

By the same token, our hymns incorporate this white supremacist notion of 'white' as a blessing. In the hymn 'Have Thine Own Way', the second stanza says,

Whiter than snow, Lord, wash me right now...

(I always ask the person standing or sitting beside me, 'Do you really want that to happen?') Similarly, the hymn 'Nothing But the Blood of Jesus', informs us that the blood of Jesus can make us 'white as snow'. (Again, I look at my pew or pulpit partner when this is sung and remark that it still hasn't worked for us.) These words have become so second nature, that when I have raised the issue with musicians and choir directors, they think I am crazy. In essence, I am arguing that unless one is aware of one's own cultural biases and interests in reading the text and appropriating the tradition, one may be seduced into adopting another's culture, one which is diametrically opposed to one's own health and well-being.

What is most discouraging in this regard is that the Black Theology movement, as a proactive response to colonialism and domination, has not impacted this aspect of our theological thinking and acting. Thus, the evidence that we are in a postcolonial situation could be debated.

III

Along with adopting the language world of the text, we have also adopted the Eurocentric reading and interpretation of the text in

many instances, so much so that we have lost our own story in the
process. In other words, we have been trained to read the stories
in ways that support the ways in which whites read them and
interpret them, which can run counter to our own psychic, spiritual, physical and emotional well-being.

One aspect of this is the ploy of the 'true' meaning of the text.
Every reader reads either from her or his own understanding of
the world, or from that of another group whose reading strategy
has been imposed upon him or her (Fish 1980; Iser 1978; Tompkins 1980). Thus, women have been trained to read stories using
the reading strategies of men, such that they root for the men,
even when the men are oppressing women. Women empathize
with Abraham over the binding of Isaac and forget this is also
Sarah's son (Exum 1993). Women identify with the spies hiding
on Rahab's roof and shun her because she is labelled a prostitute.
Women read the New Testament and don't ask why there are no
books named after women (Tolbert 1990). As Weems argues,
black women have to learn how to read 'her way' (1991).[4] Similarly, lesbians have been taught to read the book of Ruth through
heterosexist eyes and ignore the pledge Ruth makes to Naomi to
stay together until death do them part (1.16-17). In the same
manner, gay males have been taught to read David's elegy on Saul
and Jonathan, where he states Jonathan's love for him surpassed
that of a woman (2 Sam. 1.26b) to mean they had a political
alliance (Comstock 1993).

By the same token, we read the text with the interests of whites,
who are our oppressors, in mind. We, who have had our land
stolen and have been enslaved by the people who stole our land,
read the promise to Abraham to be given someone else's land and
don't see our own story. We identify with Abraham.

We have been the victims of the use of sexual innuendo. We
have been described as being more sexually endowed and active
than whites. We have been described as having more voracious
sexual appetites than they, and because of this, we have been
described as being 'animal like'. In essence, this part of the sexual

4.   I am especially indebted to these three feminist/womanist scholars for
the parallel arguments they have made in relation to feminist/womanist
readers, which I am making here in regard to race. I have been influenced
greatly by their arguments and their readings.

myth has been a lynchpin in our oppression (L. Smith 1963; Segrest 1994). It is intriguing that, when we see this type of motif used in the bible, we do not recognize our own story. We do not identify with the one or ones being maligned. Rather, we identify with the mud-slinger (Bailey 1994). When the Canaanites and Egyptians are depicted as practitioners of sexual taboos (Lev. 18.2-30), we believe this as a sanction for the holocaust of the Conquest in Joshua. Similarly, when in the Pauline and Deutero-Pauline materials, the writer goes on the attack against the enemies, be they Jews or Gentiles, the list immediately starts by labelling these people sexually. Don't be like the Gentiles, with all their 'licentiousness, greedy to practice every kind of impurity' (Eph. 4.19). Similarly, the works of the flesh are 'fornication, impurity, licentiousness...' (Gal. 5.19). By the same token the polemic against the Jews in Rom. 1.26-27 begins with 'unnatural sexual acts'. In all of these instances, the strategy of the writer is to depict the opponent as a sexually undesirable person, so that the readers will distance themselves from the opponent. Those of us who have been the victims of such strategies have been trained, however, to be alienated from our own stories and to identify with the one in charge. It is the analogy of the Native American child in the US watching a 'cowboy and Indian' movie and rooting for the cowboys.

I am suggesting that there is, on the one hand, a problem in the Eurocentric interpretation that has been rendered to the text. In many instances we have adopted those readings of the text and let them be used against ourselves. On the other hand, there are also passages in the biblical text itself, which are contrary to our experience of God, and we need to confront those with the discontinuity. In Philemon, no matter how hard Lewis (1991) helps us to see how the rhetoric of the book raises the status of Onesimus to Philemon, if we view this within the slave paradigm, as he does, Paul still sends Onesimus back. This is the ancient analogue to the Dred Scott Decision, when the US Supreme Court declared that runaway slaves had to be returned to their masters. Since Philemon is in the bible, we go through all types of mental gyrations to make it palatable, when our experience with a God of liberation would tell us that such is not of God. Such may be a polemic for liberals, who are afraid to adopt the radical options of liberation in the Jesus tradition, but such is not of the God of liberation we serve.

Similarly, Dolores Williams (1993) has helped us to reclaim Hagar in Genesis as one who meets the deity and enters into discourse. The problem is that the deity depicted in Genesis 16 tells Hagar to go back and *submit* to the oppression of Sarai. In Genesis 21 the deity depicted there tells Abraham to listen to Sarah and expel Hagar and Ishmael with bread and water. This is the depiction of a God of Oppression, not a God of Liberation. Williams calls this a God of Survival. What seems to be in play here is the need to make peace with the biblical text at all costs. Given the doctrine of the 'Word of God', we read these stories and are psychologically primed to submerge our own story and reaction to the literature and to go through mental gymnastics to redeem it (Liburd 1994). Such is also the case for Weems who resolves the tension by arguing that, when the deity asks Hagar where she is coming from and where she is going, her response only speaks of where she is coming from. Weems concludes from this that the deity has no choice but to send Hagar back (1988).

Recently, I was involved in a bible study on the Genesis 16 Hagar text at the church where I am a member. When we got to the passage where Hagar, on being pregnant, looked with contempt upon her mistress (v. 5), the women in the group understood that to mean Hagar got uppity at her ability to get pregnant, in line with traditional interpretation. I then asked how many people were or knew domestics. I then asked how many knew domestics who were raped by the man of the family with the full knowledge or even complicity of the woman of the house. People's heads started nodding. I then asked if anyone knew of women who got pregnant as a result of that rape? I then asked how they thought those women felt about the women for whom they worked. They said they were angry and despised them. I then asked how it is that we know this story from our own experience, yet we do not take that understanding to the text as we read it? I would contend that this is a vivid example of my thesis that there is a true danger in ignoring one's own cultural biases in reading and interpreting the biblical text.

IV

One of the problems in going beyond these problems is the fact that there are so few of us in the US who have doctoral degrees in the bible, and those of us who do are not necessarily doing research and publishing to move us beyond these problems. Currently, there are only 14 blacks from the US who have degrees in Hebrew Scripture, and only two are women. Similarly, there are only 14 of us in New Testament, and only one of them is a woman. Clearly, the guild has been racist and sexist in refusing to train us. Of this number, several are no longer in the academy, either due to retirement or pastoral duties in the local church. Several are still in academia but they are in administration and not involved in teaching or research. This lowers the critical mass that can help move us beyond this dilemma.

Currently, those of us who are still in academia and doing research and publishing are engaged in four different tasks. One task is the demonstration of the African presence in the text. These studies argue that 'We were there!' These studies move from conservative notions of who the African personages are, as exemplified in the works of Bennett, Copher and Martin, to claims that everyone in the text is African, except the Philistines and Greco-Romans. This type of research is seen in the *African Heritage Study Bible* (Felder 1993) and the work of Walter McCray (1991). These works take literally all references in the bible which refer to Africans (Egyptians and Cushites) and treat the text as a reliable historical document from which 'historical truth' can be discerned. For those of us who so argue, the starting point is Genesis 10, called the 'Table of Nations', and the argument is for the sons of Ham mentioned in vv. 6-8 from Egypt and Cush being black, thus securing a black presence. These studies generally, however, ignore Put, modern-day Libya and Canaan, who are also listed as 'children of Ham'.

A major goal of this type of scholarship is to build 'race pride', by arguing that we, people of African descent, were live personages in the bible. Not only that, but we were political leaders, wealthy individuals, who were positively valued in those times (Dunston 1974; Felder 1989). The basic assumption of this line of argument is that, once we realize that these characters in the bible are not white, but rather black, we will feel better about ourselves, because they are valued in the bible. In essence, they ground themselves in the 'authority of the text', as a means of pushing the race agenda.

There are several problems that are raised by both the conservative and the more extreme forms of this argument. The first is the classist nature of the argument, namely, 'We come from kings (and a few will admit queens)'. Second, these studies in most regards point to the existence of African individuals, but they do not analyze what they are doing in the text. For instance, there is little attention paid to claiming the Egyptians as black, when dealing with the Pharaonic oppression of Exodus 1–14. In these regards there is much in common with the Afrocentrism movement as exemplified by the work of Molefi Kete Asante.

Recently, there has been a move to take the question of black presence in the bible to the next level, of 'So what?' In other words, what are the characters doing there and how are they functioning literarily? Clarice Martin begins to broach this in her work on the Ethiopian in Acts 8 (1985, 1989). I have tried to do this in my work in *Stony the Road We Trod* (1991). Similarly, Renita Weems has looked at the Egyptian and Hebrew women in Exodus 1 (1992). By the same token Abraham Smith has moved forward the discussion of the literary import of the Ethiopian official in Acts 8 (1994).

A second type of scholarship being done by contemporary black biblical scholars involves the delineation of racism and white supremacy in the traditions of interpretation. Charles Copher again had done much of the spadework in this regard, especially as he traced the development of anti-black rhetoric back to rabbinic exegesis (1993). Following this trajectory in Hebrew Scripture studies is Regina Smith (1994), who has argued against white supremacist interpretations of the rhetorical question in Amos 9.7a, 'Aren't you like the Cushites to me, O, Israel?' The current main proponents of this research in New Testament studies are Clarice J. Martin (1985, 1989) and Cain Hope Felder (1989). They have been followed by Allen Callahan in a brilliant article deconstructing the 'run-away slave' interpretation of Philemon (1993). Again, such research is necessary to help us see the role of white supremacy in the formation of our understandings of the bible, but it has the effect of not taking the text itself to task, when such is a possible avenue of interpretation.

Felder has broadened his argument to make the claim that the biblical witness is one of multiculturalism and racial and ethnic toleration (1993). A major aim of this type of scholarship is to argue that the problem is not in the text, but rather that it enters with the work of the exegete or interpreter. It must be noted that the Ammonites, Moabites, Canaanites, as well as the pagans and Gentiles, would have some difficulty in accepting his argument.

In line with the above research is the interplay between racism and the other oppressive ideologies of sexism, classism and heterosexism in interpretation. As Clarice Martin has argued, we in the black church have been prepared to be somewhat progressive on the question of race, but on the issue of gender we have been most oppressive (1991). That list of oppressive variables could be extended. It appears that we are only prepared to massage our own pain and ignore that of others. We seem to want to be more than conquerors, such that we will join other oppressors, as long as the oppression is not geared towards us.

A third type of research that is being done is in the assessment and review of biblical interpretation in the history of the black community. Vincent Wimbush (1991, 1995), Renita Weems (1991) and David T. Shannon (1991) have looked through this lens. This type of research is most promising as we get a chance to see how we have read the text, in spite of what was in the text. As a furthering of this cultural-criticism approach Abraham Smith (1995) has looked at the work of Toni Morrison for clues to the ways in which African Americans have read the text and Obery Hendricks has written a most creative piece on this type of criticism (1994). A corollary to this approach is the way African scholars are looking at the similarities between traditional African mythology and the mythology of the biblical text (Oduyoye 1984; Mafico 1995). Brian Blount has also engaged in this type of criticism (1996).

A fourth type of research being done is in the area of ideological approaches, trying to discover our story and how to use it as a strategy for reading. The legitimacy of this quest, hopefully, has already been established in this endeavor. The first contemporary black biblical scholar who incorporated such a view was the black

South African scholar, Itumeleng Mosala (1989, 1992). He was
followed by Renita Weems (1992). Most recently, I have tried my
hand at such critical approaches (1994, 1995), as has Obery Hendricks (1994, 1995). This methodological approach is being
embraced by many of the new generation of black biblical scholars, who are now at the dissertation stage. Willa Johnson at
Vanderbilt is working on an examination of the expulsion of the
foreign wives and children in Ezra 9–10 and the ideology which
undergirds this text. Harold Bennet, also at Vanderbilt, is looking
at the sociology of the formula 'the stranger, orphan, and widow'
in the Deuteronomic Law Code. Similarly, Koala Jones-Warsaw
has published an article on a womanist approach to the narrative
of the Levite's concubine in Judges 19–21. Ann Holmes Redding
is deconstructing the ideology of Ephesians as expressed in the
'Household Codes', and Gay Byron is looking at Luke's treatment
of Africans in Acts. Both of these works are being done at Union
in New York.

The growing voice of black women biblical scholars is encouraging. This listing has pointed to some of those who already have
degrees, most notably, Clarice J. Martin and Renita J. Weems. It
has also noted the works of those who are on the horizon. These
individuals, some of whom are concentrating on womanist issues,
while others are concentrating on race issues, pose a necessary
corrective to the chorus.

Thus, there is hope on the horizon in the presence of black biblical scholarship which takes seriously our own cultural biases and
uses them as a guide for exegesis. In this way we can move theologically closer to an understanding of God which is not the result
of internalized oppression. Rather, these methods will lead to liberative understandings of texts which, like the spirituals, interact
with the text in powerful ways.

BIBLIOGRAPHY

Adams, D., and D. Apostolos-Cappadona
      1987   Art as Religious Studies (New York: Crossroad).
Asante, M.K.
      1987   The Afrocentric Idea (Philadelphia: Temple University).
      1988   Afrocentricity (Trenton: Africa World).
      1990   Kemet, Afrocentricity and Knowledge (Trenton: Africa World).

Ashcroft, B., G. Griffiths and H. Tiffin (eds.)
    1989   *The Empire Writes Back: Theory and Practice in Post-Colonial Literatures*
              (London: Routledge & Kegan Paul).
Bailey, R.C.
    1991   'Beyond Identification: The Use of Africans in Old Testament
              Poetry and Narratives', in Cain Hope Felder (ed.), *Stony the Road We
              Trod: African American Biblical Interpretation* (Minneapolis: Fortress
              Press): 165-84.
    1994   ' "And they shall know that I am YHWH!": The P Recasting of the
              Plague Narratives in Exodus 7–11', *JITC* 22: 1-17.
    1995a   ' "Is That Any Name for a Nice Hebrew Boy?"—Exodus 2:1-10: The
              De-Africanization of an Israelite Hero', in R.C. Bailey and J. Grant
              (eds.), *The Recovery of Black Presence: An Interdisciplinary Exploration*
              (Nashville: Abingdon Press): 25-36.
    1995b   'They're Nothing but Incestuous Bastards: The Polemical Use of
              Sex and Sexuality in Hebrew Canon Narratives', in F.F. Segovia and
              M.A. Tolbert (eds.), *Reading from This Place: Social Location and Bibli-
              cal Interpretation*, I (Minneapolis: Fortress Press): 121-38.
    1996   'Wash Me White As Snow: When Bad is Turned into Good', *Semeia*
              76: 99-113.
Bailey R.C., and T. Pippin
    1996   'Race, Class, and the Politics of Bible Translation', *Semeia* 76.
Bennett, R.A., Jr
    1971   'Africa and the Biblical Period', *HTR* 64: 501-24.
Bernal, M.
    1987   *Black Athena: The Afroasiatic Roots of Classical Civilization*, I (New
              Brunswick: Rutgers University Press).
Blount, B.
    1996   *Cultural Interpretation* (Minneapolis: Fortress Press).
Brown, R.E.
    1970   *The Gospel According to John I–XII* (AB; Garden City, NY: Doubleday).
Bultmann, R.
    1971   *The Gospel of John: A Commentary* (Philadelphia: Westminster Press).
Callahan, A.D.
    1993   'Paul's Epistle to Philemon: Toward an Alternative Argumentum',
              HTR 86: 357-76.
Comstock, G.D.
    1993   *Gay Theology without Apology* (Cleveland, OH: Pilgrim).
Cone, J.
    1975   *God of the Oppressed* (New York: Seabury).
Copher, C.B.
    1974   'The Black Man in the Biblical World', *JITC* 1: 7-16.
    1986a   'Biblical Characters, Events, Places, and Images Remembered and
              Celebrated in Black Church Worship', *JITC* 14: 75-86.
    1986b   'Three Thousand Years of Biblical Interpretation with Reference to
              Black Peoples', *JITC* 13: 225-46.
    1991   'The Black Presence in the Old Testament', in C.H. Felder (ed.),

                    Stony the Road We Trod: African American Biblical Interpretation
                    (Minneapolis: Fortress Press): 146-64.
     1993   *Black Biblical Studies: An Anthology of Charles B. Copher* (Biblical and
                    Theological Issues on the Black Presence in the Bible; Chicago:
                    Black Light Fellowship).
Costen, M.W.
     1993   *African American Christian Worship* (Nashville: Abingdon Press).
DuBois, W.E.B.
     1965   *The World and Africa: An Inquiry into the Part which Africa has Played in
                    World History* (New York: International Publishers).
Dunston, A.G.
     1974   *The Black Man in the Old Testament and its World* (Philadelphia: Dor-
                    race).
Durham, J.I.
     1987   *Exodus* (WBC, 3; Waco, TX: Word Books).
Earl. R.R., Jr
     1993   *Dark Symbols, Obscure Signs: God, Self, and Community in the Slave Mind*
                    (Maryknoll, NY: Orbis Books).
Evans, J., Jr
     1992   *We Have Been Believers: An African-American Systematic Theology*
                    (Minneapolis: Fortress Press).
Exum, J.C.
     1993   'The (M)other's Place', in *Fragmented Women: Feminist (Sub)versions of
                    Biblical Narratives* (Valley Forge, PA: Trinity).
Fanon, F.
     1963   *The Wretched of the Earth* (trans. C. Farrington; New York: Grove
                    Weidenfeld).
Felder, The Revd Cain Hope (ed.)
     1993   *The Original African Heritage Study Bible: King James Version* (Nashville:
                    James C. Winston).
Felder, The Revd Cain Hope
     1994   'Afrocentrism, the bible, and the Prophets', *PSB* 25: 131-42.
     1989   *Troubling Biblical Waters: Race, Class, and Family* (Maryknoll, NY:
                    Orbis Books).
Ferguson, G.
     1958   *Signs and Symbols in Christian Art: With Illustrations and Paintings of the
                    Renaissance* (New York: Oxford University Press).
Fish, S.
     1980   *Is There a Text in This Class? The Authority of Interpretive Communities*
                    (Cambridge, MA: Harvard University Press).
Fisher, M.M.
     1990   *Negro Slave Songs in the United States* (New York: Carol Publishing
                    Group).
Hendricks, O.
     1994   'Guerrilla Exegesis: A Post Modern Proposal for Insurgent African
                    American Biblical Interpretation', *JITC* 22: 92-109.
     1995   'A Discourse of Domination: A Socio-Rhetorical Study of the Use of
                    IUDAIOS in the Fourth Gospel' (unpublished PhD dissertation;
                    Princeton, NJ: Princeton University Press).

Hengel, M.
1974   *Judaism and Hellenism* (Philadelphia: Fortress Press).
Hood, R.E.
1990   *Must God Remain Greek? Afro Cultures and God-Talk* (Minneapolis: Fortress Press).
Hopkins, D.
1993   *Shoes That Fit our Feet: Sources for a Constructive Black Theology* (Maryknoll, NY: Orbis Books).
Hurston, Z.N.
1990   *Mules and Men* (New York: Harper & Row).
Iser, W.
1978   *The Act of Reading: A Theology of Aesthetic Response* (Baltimore: The Johns Hopkins University Press).
Jones-Warsaw, K.
1993–94   'Towards a Womanist Hermeneutic: A Reading of Judges 19–21', in A. Brenner (ed.), *A Feminist Companion to Judges* (The Feminist Companion to the Bible, 4; Sheffield: Sheffield Academic Press): 172-86; also in *JITC* 22: 18-35.
Käsemann, E.
1969   *Jesus Means Freedom* (Philadelphia: Fortress Press).
Lewis, L.A.
1991   'An African American Appraisal of the Philemon–Paul–Onesimus Triangle', in C.H. Felder (ed.), *Stony the Road We Trod: African American Biblical Interpretation* (Minneapolis: Fortress Press): 232-46.
Liburd, R.
1994   ' "Like...a House upon the Sand": African American Biblical Hermeneutics in Perspective', *JITC* 22: 71-91.
Lincoln, C.E.
1978   'White Christianity and Black Commitment: A Comment on the Power of Faith and Socialization', *JITC* 6: 21-31.
Lincoln, C.E., and L.H. Mamiya
1990   *The Black Church in the African American Experience* (Durham: Duke University Press).
Lovell, J.
1972   *Black Song: The Forge and Flame* (New York: Macmillan).
Mafico, T.L.J.
1995   'The Divine Name Yahweh 'Elohim from an African Perspective', in F.F. Segovia and M.A. Tolbert (eds.), *Reading from This Place: Social Location and Biblical Interpretation in Global Perspective*, II (Minneapolis: Fortress Press).
Martin, C.J.
1985   'The Function of Acts 8:26-40 within the Narrative Structure of the Book of Acts: The Significance of the Eunuch's Provenance for Acts 1:8c' (unpublished PhD dissertation; Durham: Duke University Press).
1989   'A Chamberlain's Journey and the Challenge of Interpretation for Liberation', *Semeia* 47: 105-35.

1991   'The *Haustafeln* (Household Codes) in African American Biblical
            Interpretation: "Free Slaves" and "Subordinated Women"', in C.H.
            Felder (ed.), *Stony the Rod We Trod: African American Biblical Interpre-
            tation* (Minneapolis: Fortress Press): 206-31.

McCray, W.
1991   *The Black Presence in the Bible* (Chicago: Black Light).

Morris, L.
1971   *The Gospel According to John* (NICNT; Grand Rapids: Eerdmans).

Mosala, I.J.
1989   *Biblical Hermeneutics and Black Theology in South Africa* (Grand Rapids:
            Eerdmans).
1992   'The Implications of the Text of Esther for African Women's Strug-
            gle for Liberation in South Africa', *Semeia* 59: 129-37.

Oduyoye, M.
1984   *The Sons of the Gods and the Daughters of Men: An Interpretation of Gene-
            sis 1–11* (Maryknoll, NY: Orbis Books).

Owens, J.G.
1971   *All God's Chillun: Meditations on Negro Spirituals* (Nashville: Abingdon
            Press).

Piper, D.
1991   *The Illustrated History of Art* (New York: Crescent Books).

Raboteu, A.
1978   *Slave Religion: The 'Invisible Institution' in the Antebellum South* (New
            York: Oxford University Press).
1995   *A Fire in the Bones: Reflections on African American Religious History*
            (Boston: Beacon Press).

Rensberger, D.
1988   *Johannine Faith and Liberating Community* (Philadelphia: Westminster
            Press).

Segrest, M.
1994   *Memoir of a Race Traitor* (Boston: South End).

Servett, M.C. (ed.)
1985   *Afro-American Religious History: A Documentary Witness* (Durham: Duke
            University Press).

Shannon, D.T.
1991   '"An Ante-bellum Sermon": A Resource for an African American
            Hermeneutic', in C.H. Felder (ed.), *Stony the Road We Trod: African
            American Biblical Interpretation* (Minneapolis: Fortress Press): 98-123.

Smith, A.
1994   '"Do You Understand What You are Reading?': A Literary Critical
            Reading of the Ethiopian (Kushite) Episode (Acts 8:26-40)', *JITC*
            22: 48-70.
1995   'Toni Morrison's Song of Solomon: The Blues and the bible', in
            R.C. Bailey and J. Grant (eds.), *The Recovery of Black Presence: An
            Interdisciplinary Exploration* (Nashville: Abingdon Press): 107-15.

Smith, L.
1963   *Killers of the Dream* (Garden City, NY: Anchor, 2nd edn rev. and
            enl.).

Smith, R.
    1994   'A New Perspective on Amos 9:7', *JITC* 22: 36-47.
Smith, T.
    1994   *Conjuring Culture: Biblical Formations of Black America* (New York: Oxford University Press).
Spivak, G.C.
    1993   'The Politics of Translation', in *idem, Outside in the Teaching Machine* (London: Routledge & Kegan Paul).
Thurman, H.
    1975   *Deep River and the Negro Spiritual Speaks of Life and Death* (Richmond, IN: Friends United).
    1981   *With Head and Heart: The Autobiography of Howard Thurman* (New York: Harper & Row).
    1996   *Jesus and the Disinherited* (Boston: Beacon Press).
Tolbert, M.A.
    1990   'Protestant Women and Feminism: On the Horns of a Dilemma', in A. Bach (ed.), *The Pleasure of her Text: Feminist Readings of Biblical and Historical Texts* (Philadelphia: Trinity Press): 5-24.
Tompkins, J.P. (ed.)
    1980   *Reader-Response: From Formalism to Post-Structuralism* (Baltimore: The Johns Hopkins University Press).
Townes, E.M. (ed.)
    1993   *A Troubling in my Soul: Womanist Perspectives On Evil and Suffering* (Maryknoll, NY: Orbis Books).
Van Sertima, I.
    1976   *They Came before Columbus: The African Presence in Ancient America* (New York: Random House).
Walker, D.
    1965   *David Walker's Appeal (1819)* (ed. C.M. Wiltse; New York: Hill & Wang [1819]).
Watts, J.D.W.
    1987   *Isaiah 34–66* (WBC, 25; Waco, TX: Word Books).
Weems, R.J.
    1988   *Just a Sister Away: A Womanist Vision of Women's Relationships in the Bible* (San Diego: Lura Media).
    1991   'Reading her Way through the Struggle: African American Women and the Bible', in C.H. Felder (ed.), *Stony the Road We Trod: African American Biblical Interpretation* (Minneapolis: Fortress Press): 57-77.
    1992   'The Hebrew Women Are Not Like the Egyptian Women: The Ideology of Race, Gender, and Sexual Reproduction in Exodus 1', *Semeia* 59: 25-34.
Williams, D.
    1993   *Sisters in the Wilderness: The Challenge of Womanist God-Talk* (Maryknoll, NY: Orbis Books).
Wilmore, G.S.
    1983   *Black Religion and Black Radicalism: An Interpretation of the Religious History of Afro-American People* (Maryknoll, NY: Orbis Books, 2nd edn).

Wimbush, V.L.
    1991   'The Bible and African Americans: An Outline of Interpretive
                History', in C.H. Felder (ed.), *Stony the Road We Trod: African Ameri-
                can Biblical Interpretation* (Minneapolis: Fortress Press): 81-97.
    1995   'Reading Texts as Reading Ourselves: A Chapter in the History of
                African-American Biblical Interpretation', in F.F. Segovia and M.A.
                Tolbert (eds.), *Reading from This Place: Social Location and Biblical
                Interpretation in the United States,* I (Minneapolis: Fortress Press): 95-
                108.
Wood, W.
    1994   *Keep the Faith Baby* (Oxford: Bible Reading Fellowship).

A Postcolonial Exploration of Collusion and Construction in Biblical Interpretation

R S. SUGIRTHARAJAH

> 'Easy win, monkey,' Ganesh said. 'The old fellow's education is so
> much deeper.'
> 'Ah, yes, but the Bengali's reading is so much wider,' Hanuman
> said. 'He has an MA in colonial literature.'
> 'True, true, but that will apply only peripherally, if at all.'
> Vikram Chandra, *Red Earth and Pouring Rain*

I set out to do three things in this essays. First, to trace the emergence of postcolonialism as a critical discourse and then to try to define postcolonialism. Second, I shall examine the collusion between colonialism and exegesis, and contest the Eurocentric construction of Christian origins. To illustrate the former, I shall revisit two key mission narratives, the Great Commission (Mt. 28.19) and Paul's missionary tours (Acts 13–14; 15.40–18.22; 18.22–21.16) and demonstrate how the Matthaean verse was reactivated and the Pauline missionary-journey pattern was fabricated at the time of Western colonial expansion with the busy involvement of Western mercantile companies. Third, and to elucidate the latter, I shall look at the formation of the gospel tradition and the reluctance and shyness on the part of Western biblical critics to admit any interfusion of Eastern conceptual categories into the gospel materials. In conclusion, as an exercise in clarification, for those who are engaged in postcolonial reading practice, I should like to set out some of the issues we now need to address.

Postcolonialism emerged as a critical activity within what is known as Commonwealth or Third World Literature Studies. As the Indian critic Harish Trivedi claims, it was the first time that the colonized other was placed at the centre of academic discourse:

> Unlike with feminism or post-structuralism or even Marxism, the
> discourse of post-colonialism is ostensibly not about the West
> where it has originated but about the colonised other. For the first
> time probably in the whole history of the Western academy, the
> non-West is placed at the centre of its dominant discourse. Even if
> it is in part a sort of compensation for all the colonial material
> exploitation, the academic attention now being paid to the post-
> colonial is so assiduous as to soothe and flatter (1996: 232).

He also goes on to warn that this new attention, a grudging favour
granted by the West, could well be a new form of colonialism.

Since the 1960s, most of the literary productions which
emerged during and after colonialism in the former colonies in
Asia and Africa, were accorded the title 'Commonwealth Literature'. The term 'Commonwealth' not only kept alive the notion of
British cultural influence, but also perpetuated the notion that
the empire had been a willing association of free people.
Recently, the term 'postcolonialism' has been used increasingly to
signify the text and context of these writings. Postcolonialism got
its imprimatur when the publishers Routledge, at the last minute,
changed the name of a volume which had been under prepara-
tion for more than a decade from *The Encyclopedia of Commonwealth Literature* to *The Encyclopedia of Postcolonial Literatures in
English* (M. Mukherjee 1996: 5). A further important moment in
postcolonial discourse was the production of the Indian series
Subaltern Studies: Writings on South Asian History and Society.
This dissident project, in keeping with the efforts of the radical
movements of the 1970s to write history from the underside, has
been successful in scrutinizing, challenging and transforming how
the subaltern was constructed in the dominant models of Indian
historiography.[1] We also need to recognize the outstanding work
of C.L.R. James, Franz Fanon, Aime Cesaire, Amilcar Cabral,
Albert Memmi, Chinua Achebe and Ngugi wa Thiongo, to a name
a few, whose writings, though emanating from diverse cultural
and historical locations, offered precursory intellectual stimulus
to the current postcolonial thinking.

Initially, postcolonialism was seen as a convenient pedagogical
tool rather than as advancing particular theoretical concepts. It

---

1.   So far there have been nine volumes published, under the editorship
of different authors, by Oxford University Press, Delhi.

was later that cultural critics like Edward Said (1985, 1993), Spivak (1988, 1990) and Homi Bhabha (1994) gave postcolonialism its theorization and practice. This trio speaks from different sites, and mobilizes different philosophical and conceptual categories. Their writings resist any neat summary, yet there is a certain central aspect and unifying force in their approach, namely, to investigate and expose the link between knowledge and power in the textual production of the West. One can detect at least two meanings and usages of postcolonialism emerging from their writings—postcolonialism as reading strategy, and as a state or a condition. Said and Spivak treat postcolonialism as a reading strategy. Bhabha, on the other hand, sees postcoloniality as a condition of being. He foregrounds the contemporary subjectivities in literary and epistemological terms, at the same time highlighting the issues of ambivalence and hybridity.

Postcolonialism is not simply a physical expulsion of imperial powers. Nor is it simply recounting the evils of the empire, and drawing a contrast with the nobility and virtues of natives and their cultures. Rather, it is an active confrontation with the dominant system of thought, its lopsidedness and inadequacies, and underlines its unsuitability for us. Hence, it is a process of cultural and discursive emancipation from all dominant structures whether they be political, linguistic or ideological.

Postcolonialism, it has to be stressed, has a multiplicity of meanings, depending on location. It is seen as an oppositional reading practice, and as a way of critiquing the totalizing forms of Eurocentric thinking and of reshaping dominant meanings. It is a mental attitude rather than a method, more a subversive stance towards the dominant knowledge than a school of thought. It is not about periodization. It is a reading posture. It is a critical enterprise aimed at unmasking the link between idea and power, which lies behind Western theories and learning. It is a discursive resistance to imperialism, imperial ideologies, imperial attitudes and their continued incarnations in such wide-ranging fields as politics, economics, history and theological and biblical studies.

An anti-colonial mode of critique is not new. There were earlier attempts during the colonial days. In confronting the colonizer, the earlier colonized in the Raj era made use of the Western constructions of the colonizer and the colonized, of centre and

periphery. The earlier colonized were largely shaped by, and
remained in many ways locked into, the very structure they were
keen on demolishing. What is new in the current anti-imperial
contestation is that it goes beyond the essentialist and contrastive
ways of thinking, East–West, us–them, vernacular–metropolitan,
and seeks a radical syncretizing of each opposition. Where the
current postcolonialism differs from the earlier form is that while
challenging the oppressive nature of colonialism it recognizes the
potentiality of contact between colonizer and colonized. Distanc-
ing itself from both the reverent admiration of native values and a
cringing attitude towards all that is Western, the present postcolonialism tries to integrate and forge a new perspective by critically and profitably syncretizing ingredients from both vernacular
and metropolitan centres.

Postcolonialism as a critical enterprise is, in Samia Mehrez's
view, an 'act of exorcism' for both the colonized and the colonizer. 'For both parties it must be a process of liberation: from
dependency, in the case of the colonized, and from imperialist,
racist perceptions, representations, and institutions which, unfortunately, remain with us till this very day, in the case of the colonizer' (1991: 258). In other words, in the process of decolonization, the imperializer and the imperialized are inevitably locked
together. In the case of the former, it means re-examining their
collusion with the empire and imperialism, and reassessing a
Western ethnocentrism which was passed off as universalism. In
the case of the latter, it means reviewing internal colonization,
virulent forms of nationalism and excessive nativism.

One of the hermeneutical agendas in this liberative role of
postcolonialism is to encourage what Edward Said calls
'contrapuntal reading'. This is a reading strategy advocated by
him with a view to encouraging the experiences of the exploited
and the exploiter to be studied together. In other words, texts
from metropolitan centres and peripheries are studied simultaneously. Contrapuntal reading paves the way for a situation which
goes beyond reified binary characterizations of Eastern and Western writings. To read contrapuntally means to be aware simultaneously of mainstream scholarship and of other scholarship which
the dominant discourse tries to domesticate and speaks and acts
against. In Said's words, 'we…re-read it not univocally but con-

trapuntally, with a simultaneous awareness both of the metropolitan history that is narrated and of those other histories against which (and beyond which) the dominating discourse acts' (1993: 59). Translating this into the biblical field, it means to read Hisako Kinukawa's, *Women and Jesus in Mark* with Bas van Iersel's *Reading Mark*; Karl Barth's *Romans* with Tamez's *The Amnesty of Grace: Justification by Faith from a Latin American Perspective*; Bultmann's *John* with Appasamy's *Christianity as Bhakti Marga*; and Neil Elliot's *Liberating Paul: The Justice of God and the Politics of the Apostle* with Jaswant Raj's *Grace in the Saiva Siddhantham and in St Paul*. By linking such works to each other, and juxtaposing neglected texts with the mainstream, we can highlight gaps, absences and imbalances.

Mandating Mission and Imperialism

Both as a state or a condition, and as a reading strategy, postcolonialism is a useful critical concept for New Testament studies. In this regard, a preliminary task will be to disrupt some of the prevailing assumptions about the New Testament. As an example, I should like to reinvestigate some of the texts and exegetical practices which undergirded and colluded with colonialism and colonial mission. I am particularly interested in looking again at the Matthaean missionary commission (Mt. 28.19) and the missionary journeys of Paul (Acts 13–14; 15.40–18.22; 18.22–21.16). These were profitably used in the missionary efforts of the church in the colonial period. Commentaries for Indian students written during both the colonial and the post-independent periods, mobilized Matthew's text as a biblical warrant to missionize the natives, and utilized the mission-journey narratives, as a model for their Christianizing work. These texts had been dormant and were largely disregarded by the reformers, yet were reinvoked in the eighteenth and nineteenth centuries during the evangelical revival which significantly coincided with the rise of Western imperialism. At this time, the Matthaean text came to be used as a template to institutionalize the missionary obligation, and Luke's alleged recording of Paul's missionary undertaking was fabricated as a way of perpetuating the myth that it was from the West that the superstitious and ignorant natives received the essential verities of God's message.

Before the eighteenth century, Matthew's command 'Go ye and preach' was an unfashionable, under-exegeted, often even absent, text. It was William Carey (1761–1834), the Baptist missionary pioneer, who reactivated it as a missionary command for the modern period.[2] The earlier missionaries seem to have appealed to and sought endorsement from other texts. Robert de Nobili (1577–1656) found the Pauline axiom 'to the Jews I have become a Jew' spurring him on in his missionary endeavours in South India (Neill 1934: 56). Frederick Schwartz (1726–98) recuperated another Matthaean verse: 'Come unto me all ye that labour and are heavy laden, I will give you rest' (11.25) (Page 1921: 56), and the first English mission agency, the Society for the Propagation of the Gospel in Foreign Parts, founded in 1701, sent its first missionaries to America on the basis of the appeal in Acts, 'Come over...and help us' (Thompson 1951: 19). David Bosch furnishes a further list of texts exemplifying the missionary thrust in different periods of history. The patristic understanding of mission was based on Jn 3.16, whereas the medieval Roman Catholic missionary impulse was animated by Lk. 14.23: 'Go out to the highways and hedges, compel people to come in, that my house may be filled.' The Reformers looked to Rom. 1.16-17. The Enlightenment era produced its own host of preferential texts. The aforementioned Acts 16.9 had been prominent among Western Christians who saw their task as rescuing the peoples in distant lands who were in darkness. The premillenialists mandated their mission in the words of Jesus: 'And this gospel of the kingdom will be preached throughout the whole world, as a testimony to all nations; and then the end will come' (Mt. 24.14); and the Social Gospellers appealed to the Johannine saying: 'I came that they may have life, and have it abundantly' (Jn 10.10) (Bosch 1991: 339-40).

Carey, on the other hand, in his pamphlet, *An Enquiry into the Obligations of Christians to Use Means for the Conversion of the Heathen* (1792), resurrected the Matthaean commission as the proof text for compulsive preaching of the gospel in distant lands. The *Enquiry*, a curious text for its time, resembles the prospectus of a modern-day multinational company, with elaborate statistical details reminding Christians of their inescapable obligation to

2.   See Boer (1961: 16, 17).

preach the gospel to distant lands. The pamphlet was not only a missionary apologetic but provided a strategy as well. Central to all this was Mt. 28.19. Since then, this verse has exercised a considerable influence on the institutionalized missionary efforts of the Christian church.

The phenomenal expansion of Christianity in the first few centuries seems on the whole to have come about with little institutionalized mission and little formal preaching. Alan Kreider, who has investigated the growth of the pre-Christendom church, is of the view that organized mission played little part in its expansion:

> [T]here was, as Arthur Darby Nock has emphasised, 'little, if any direct preaching to the masses'; it was simply too dangerous. Or organizing the congregations for mission: according to Georg Kretschmar, 'the recruitment to the faith was never institutionalized'... How about prayer for the conversion of pagans? According to Yves Congar, 'the Christians prayed for the prosperity and peace of people, but scarcely for their conversion'. Most of the very few prayers for conversion which survive from the early centuries, eight out of eleven in all according to my count, are in fact prayers in obedience to Jesus' command to pray for enemies and persecutors. As to theologizing of an explicitly missionary nature, the only word which for Norbert Brox will adequately describe 'the scarcity of reflection about mission' is 'astonishing'. To this list of surprising omissions I would like to add one more. In my reading of early Christian materials with a missionary's eyes, I have been amazed at the absence of pastoral admonitions to evangelise. A sample of this is *Ad Quirinum* by the North African bishop and martyr Cyprian. The third book of this work is a manual of 120 'heavenly precepts' to guide catechumens in the Christian life. These 'precepts' cover a whole range of areas of Christian concern—'that brethren ought to support one another', or 'that we are to be urgent in prayers'— but none, not one of the 120, urges the believers to evangelise (1994: 8).

He goes on to furnish the actual reasons for the growth of the early Jesus movement. The movement grew in the early days not because there was organized oral dissemination of God's word, but through public demonstration of the faith. This was mediated by a number of means. For instance, martyrdom, which brought not only notoriety but also admiration for a people who valued their new-found faith and were willing to die for it. People also came to know about the new faith in less dramatic ways.

Exemplary behaviour of individual Christians at workplaces and in neighbourhoods attracted attention. Exorcism, too, played a vital evangelistic part: 'in an age of competitive miracle-working, the Christian God seemed stronger than other Gods' (Kreider 1994: 12). In Kreider's view Christianity also spread in the pre-Christendom phase because of the extraordinary characteristics of Christian worship, which nurtured and prepared Christians to face the outside world: 'The worship was shaping a people whose life, and whose response to the world, were distinctive' (28).

In contrast with the movement described by Kreider, Protestant Christianity was strikingly inert in Carey's England. Indeed, it was a Roman Catholic argument against the Reformation that it had failed to inspire mission. The title of the first section of Carey's pamphlet 'An Enquiry Whether the Commission given by Our Lord to his Disciples be not still binding on us' is an indication of the hermeneutical mood of the time:

> There seems also to be an opinion existing in the minds of some, that because the apostles were extraordinary officers and have no proper successors, and because many things which were right for them to do would be utterly unwarrantable for us, therefore it may not be immediately binding on us to execute the commission, though it was so upon them (Carey 1961: 8).

Carey, in summoning Matthew's closing verses, was countering the prevalent hermeneutical convention of his time. For instance, the view among the Danish clergy of the time was that no further worldwide mission was called for. This, they based on their reading of Rom. 10.18 and Col. 1.23. These verses were interpreted to mean that the apostles had preached the Gospel to 'every creature under heaven' (Sandgren 1991: 83). Thus, for the Reformers and for the ecclesiastical thinkers of Carey's time, the commission had been binding only on the apostles and had lost its efficacy with their death. The Reformers did not envision an organized missionary programme, and took it for granted that they did not have a mandate to preach the gospel and to establish churches in distant places. Such a perception was based on the Reformers' understanding of ecclesiastical duties. They distinguished between two kinds of offices—apostles and pastors. It had been the task of the former to preach everywhere they went, and the latter's role was to serve the local churches, their authority limited to the area of their ministry. Calvin encapsulated this thinking when he wrote:

> ...for the Lord created the apostles, that they might spread the gospel throughout the whole world, and he did not assign to each of them certain limits or parishes, but would have them, wherever they went, to discharge the office of ambassadors among all nations and languages. In this respect there is a difference between them and pastors, who are, in a manner, tied to their particular churches. For the pastor has not a commission to preach the gospel over the whole world, but to take care of the Church that has been committed to his charge (cited in Boer 1961: 19).

Luther, too, held similar views.[3] Though he rediscovered the power of the Word, he continued to subscribe to the received notion that missionary preaching was a privilege of the apostles. Carey, a Baptist and Calvinist, was reacting against this Reformation understanding when he reappropriated the Great Commission.

Carey's hermeneutical challenge to the received missiological orthodoxy of the earlier phase of European colonialism and imperialism invites a further postcolonial reconsideration, and a first question might be whether the Matthaean church was true to the great commission or whether there is any sign of its members having engaged in missionary activities? The popular perception of the Matthaean community has been that it had a positive Gentile bias and was actively involved in evangelizing them. A fresh investigation by David C. Sim contests such assumptions (1995). He has shown that there is internal and external evidence to suggest the contrary. The Gospel of Matthew contains a number of unsympathetic statements about the Gentiles (5.46-47; 6.7-8, 31-32; 18.15-17). It is not always generous to those who were not part of the Jewish race. They are called 'dogs' and deemed not worthy to eat the bread that belonged to the children of Israel. The strongest contempt for Gentiles was expressed in Mt. 18.17, where Matthew's Jesus instructed the followers that if a wrongdoer failed to accept the correction of the community then that person should be treated 'as a Gentile and a tax collector'. The disciples are also instructed not to follow the example of the Gentiles in seeking position and power (Mt. 10.25). The writer of

3.   See Boer (1961: 19).

Matthew's Gospel did not think much of Gentile piety either. In his reckoning the prayer of the Gentile was a vain noise (Mt. 6.7). These negative perceptions indicate that for Matthew the Gentile world is a foreign and godless place which must be avoided and, more importantly, whose practices must not be imitated by his readers. The reason for this stance could be attributed to the per-secution the Matthaean community faced at the hands of the Gentiles during and following the first Jewish war against Rome. Matthew's discourses on mission (ch. 10) and apocalypticism (chs. 24–25) corroborate this.

What is interesting is that Carey's call to win the souls of the unbelievers in foreign lands and his reactivating of the Matthaean command happened at a time of unprecedented territorial con-quest by the West. Historians of colonialism have come up with different periodizations of the imperial advance of the West. Carey's call to evangelize distant lands falls within what Marc Ferro categorizes as colonialism of a new type, yoked to the Indus-trial Revolution and to financial capitalism, and marked by expansionist policies (1997: 19). It is highly significant to a post-colonial hermeneutic that Carey's fascination with this dormant verse arose at a time when Europe was engaged in just such a colonialism.

This leads us nicely to the missionary tours of Paul, and it will become clear as we go along that the reconfiguration of the tour scheme, too, had interlocked with the imperial advance of Europe.

Missionary Tours and Mercantile Trading Companies

The emergence of many missionary societies in the eighteenth and nineteenth centuries led exegetes to impose a missionary-journey structure on the Acts. This missionary-tour scheme has been used to sustain and legitimize mission activity. Generations of Indian students studying for the Serampore theological degree[4] have been asked to answer a question which runs like this:

---

4.   Serampore College, the first Western-style college in Asia, is the only Protestant institution which has a charter to confer theological degrees in India. It is proud of the fact that it got its charter from Denmark in 1818, even before the University of Calcutta was instituted.

'Describe the missionary journeys of Paul and draw out the implications for the missionary task in today's India.' The textbooks available offered ample scholarly help to the hapless students. There were two commentary series specifically written for Indian students—the Indian Church Commentaries and the Christian Students' Library.[5] The commentaries on Acts in both series contain a plan of the book. In this, the commentators make the three journeys central to Luke's volume. Harold Moulton, one of those who contributed to the Christian Students' Library, wrote: 'Most of the remainder of the book is taken up with the account of the missionary tours designed to plant the Gospel in the places where it can have most effect if it strikes root' (1957: 40). He persuades the students: 'the same strategic sense is necessary for the full development of the Christian enterprise everywhere' (41). A similar view is expressed by T. Walker who contributed a volume for the other series: '[Acts is] in the main, a record of mission work in distant lands' (1919: lii). He goes on to say that the very divisions of the book emphasize this fact, and 'follow the lines of the Saviour's last command' (lv). Moulton also concocted a missionary headquarters, Jerusalem/Antioch, to which Paul keeps returning and reporting (55, 57).

Like the missionary command, the tour scheme had been paid little attention by either the pre-Christendom church or the Reformers. The first reference to the journey pattern, according to John Townsend, appeared in J.A. Bengel's *Gnomon Novi Testamenti* (1742). Even here Bengel mentioned it only in his preface and failed to follow this up in his commentary or in the chronology of Paul that he published separately. The commentaries which followed the work of Bengel also adopted the mission-journey pattern. Surveying the commentarial writings on Acts in early and medieval times, Townsend concludes that the writers were silent about the missionary pattern. Ancient writers such as Irenaeus, Jerome, Ephraem, John Chrysostom and Bede observe a hermeneutical reticence on this topic: 'The fact that these writers ... are silent about a missionary-journey pattern in Acts would certainly cast doubt on any argument that the pattern was originally

5.   For a postcolonial critique of these series, see Sugirtharajah forthcoming 2.

intended by the author of Luke–Acts' (1986: 102). This is equally true of those who belonged to a later time, Erasmus, Calvin and Theodore Beza, who failed to detect in Acts the missionary itinerary.

A rereading of the textual evidence in Acts raises a serious challenge to the accepted view that the author conceived a triple journey plan for Paul with Antioch or Jerusalem providing the base for departure and return. Of the three journeys, only the first (chs. 13–14) has some semblance of a missionary tour, originating from Antioch. It takes Paul through Cyprus and a series of towns of Southern Asia Minor—Pisidian Antioch, Iconium, Lystra and Derbe—and then he goes back by the same route but missing out Cyprus. The 'second journey' seems have been unplanned, and Paul simply drifts from one Roman city to another, until he reaches Corinth and settles down there for a while, getting involved in a fracas with the local Jewish community. He decides to leave, and the 'third' tour begins at once, at 18.23. It is a misnomer even to call it a journey because Paul spends three years in Ephesus (20.31)—three months in the synagogue (19.8) and two years in the school of Tyrannus (19.10) debating. It was during this time that he was involved in the Corinthian correspondence, and, according to 2 Cor. 13.2, in an unhappy and unprofitable trip to Corinth. He returns to Ephesus and then moves up to Macedonia and then to Greece, or probably Corinth, where he spends three months, followed by a short stay in Troas (20.6-12); and then journeys down the west coast of Asia Minor, finally reaching Jerusalem. Interestingly, the *Acts of Paul*, an early Christian text which describes Paul's work and travels, does not seem to be aware of such a tour pattern, but instead sees his travels through various Roman cities as a 'single continuous journey without a return to some sponsoring Church' (Townsend 1986: 101). Roland Allen, too, who drew on Paul and worked out a model for conducting missions in the foreign field, is doubtful about a planned scheme: 'It is quite impossible to maintain that St Paul deliberately planned his journeys before hand, selected certain strategic points at which to establish his Churches and then actually carried out his designs' (1912: 15).

Why, then, was a missionary pattern imposed on the Acts during the colonial period? The likely answer is that the commentators were swayed by the momentous territorial changes taking place at the time, and were reading these events back into Apostolic times. The eighteenth century witnessed the rise of Western Protestant missionary activity and the establishment of a plethora of denominational missionary agencies. From the Protestant side, the Society for the Promotion of Christian Knowledge was founded in 1698; the Baptist Missionary Society in 1792; the London Missionary Society in 1795; the Church Missionary Society in 1799; the Wesleyan Methodist Society in 1813; and the Netherlands Missionary Society in 1797. Roman Catholic mission activity in the modern period goes back to the formation of the Sacra de Propaganda Fide in 1662, and further impetus was given by the founding of the Association for the Propagation of the Faith in 1822.

> Unlike the earlier missionaries, such as Francis Xavier (1506–52), who had wandered about fairly much on their own, missionaries of this period looked to their home societies for support and guidance in their work. Since it was standard missionary practice for evangelists to operate out of a home base, one should not be surprised at the exegetical assumption that Paul, the great missionary of the New Testament, had done the same (Townsend 1986: 104).

It is no coincidence that the founding of all these missionary societies took place contemporaneously with the activities of trading companies like the East India Company and the Dutch East India Company. The East India Company initially resisted the presence of the missionaries. It feared that the interference of missionaries in local religious customs and manners might be counter-productive to its mercantile interests. However, with the renewal of the Company's charter in 1833 and the abolition of its monopoly, missionary enterprise received a boost. It was further helped by the British Indian Government's legislature, which set out to protect the rights of the Christian converts. Once the impediment to missionary work was removed, the missionaries themselves became willing supporters of commercial expansion. William Ward (1769–1823), the colleague of Carey at Serampore in India, lamented the 'extraordinary fact' that the British goods purchased annually by India were 'not sufficient to freight a single vessel from our ports'. But he hoped that once Indians were enlightened and civilized they would 'contribute more to the real prosperity of Britain as a commercial people, by consuming her

manufactures to a vast extent'. He went on: 'But let the Hindoost-
'han receive that higher civilization she needs, that cultivation of
which she is so capable; let European literature be transfused into
all her languages, then the ocean from the ports of Britain to
India, will be covered with our merchant vessels…' (1820: liii).
When the Opium War ended and the Nanking Treaty favoured
Western trade and missions to China, a Swedish pastor who was
monitoring the news in the East wrote: 'Trade shall be a vehicle
for mission' (Sundkler 1965: 121). Mission and mercantile interest often overlapped.

   In concluding this section, some reflections. The trouncing of
the Spanish Armada by the English had a major impact on
geopolitics and mission. Previously, mission could be carried on
only under the auspices of one or other of the colonial powers;
these, however, were all Catholic (Sundkler 1965: 97). With
Catholic maritime control loosened, the way was cleared for
Protestant England and Holland, with their newly rediscovered
Bible, to enter the fray. Along with the scramble for territories
arose also a sense of missionary obligation (Sundkler 1965: 97),
while, significantly, as we have seen, conditions created by Protestant Europe's maritime access to overseas colonies informed biblical interpretation. The rise of Protestant countries as colonial
powers, the vigorous mushrooming of Protestant mission-sending
agencies, and the recuperation of missionary texts, were all inex-
tricably mixed.

   The story of the expansion of the church as it is told through
Paul's journeys in Acts is selective and partial. It documents only
the spreading of the church in the West and totally ignores the
Eastward movement of the church. It celebrates and privileges
only the Hellenistic expansion of the church, namely, from
Jerusalem to Rome, and the Jewish mission to Gentiles in the
Roman Empire. What the author of Acts fails to record is that
there was another history of the founding of the church east of
the Euphrates and throughout the Persian Empire, whose territorial control extended to the borders of India. While Paul and
other Christians were engaged in mission among Greeks, Romans
and barbaric tribes in the West, the people of the East, especially
in Edessa, Persia, Arabia and Central Asia, China and India, were
also being presented with the message:

> It is a surprise to most people to learn that there was a large and
> wide-spread Christian community throughout the whole of Central
> Asia in the first centuries of the present era and that such countries
> as Afghanistan and Tibet which are spoken of to-day as lands
> closed to the gospel message were centres of Christian activity long
> before Mohammed was born or the Krishna legend had been
> heard of (Stewart 1928: xxix-xxx).

The missionary impulse for the spread of Christianity in Asia,
according to T.V. Philip came not from Hellenistic but from
Jewish Christianity (1997). As with the case of the westward
expansion of the Church, the eastward spread too was achieved
not through institutionalized preaching but through the effective
presence of Christians. The monastic movement and its ascetic
ideals played a considerable role:

> The monks were popular with the masses... The masses knew that
> the monks had particular compassion to those who suffered and
> the monks were always willing to help the people spiritually as well
> as materially. The monasteries became congregating centres of the
> poor and those who suffered (Philip 1997: 12).

Traders, craftspeople, migrants and refugees from religious per-
secution all carried the gospel. It is this story of the eastward
expansion which has been totally ignored in the narration of
Luke–Acts. Philip reminds historians of mission to look again at
*The Odes of Solomon, The Gospel of Thomas, The Acts of Judas Thomas,
Didascalia Apostolorum*, and the writings of Ephraem, Aphrahat
and Narsai, to understand the movement of Christianity to the
East (1997: 8).

The imposition of a missionary-tour pattern on Acts has other
hermeneutical implications in addition to bolstering a westward
expansion of the church. It reinforces the view that the churches
in Asia and Africa have been recipients of the gospel as a gift from
a benevolent West to enlighten the heathen. It largely ignores the
Christian presence in these parts of the world before the arrival of
the modern missionary movement. John England in his recent
book *The Hidden History of Christianity in Asia* (1996) has traced the
often-ignored and seldom-discussed complex and diverse histories
of the church in Asia. He attributes such neglect to, among other
things: 'Outdated assumptions regarding orthodoxy and heresy,
along with culturally-confined criteria in scholarship... [which]

often prevent any adequate study of eastern Christianity in terms of its own historical and cultural setting' (pp. 2, 3). Drawing on a variety of evidence ranging from manuscripts to coins and paintings, he has demonstrated that it is possible to establish the presence of Christians from 'Syria in the west to Japan in the northeast and as far as Java in the south-east by the first half of the eighth century' (p. 8). The perception held hitherto of the post-Nicene history of European peoples as normative, is, in England's view, now, with the availability of the 'equally rich history of east of Antioch', unsustainable.

The hermeneutical concoction of a missionary headquarters to which Paul keeps returning after completing an assignment is a critical one. Since most of the modern movement's missionaries worked with and through a home base in Europe, and were constantly in touch with them regarding the running of the native churches, the origins of such an exegetical conjecture are clear (Townsend 1986: 104). But the implication for churches in Asia or for that matter Africa or the Pacific is significant. The idea of a headquarters, be it in London, Halle or Geneva, takes on a different shading. Besides the suggestion of the organizational power and institutional might of the gospel, encoded in the word 'headquarters', is the idea that there is over there a large and controlling decision-making machinery. Anything these churches do has to be checked and validated by an external authority.

Carey's contemporaries were Tom Paine and Mary Wollstonecraft. Wollstonecraft's *The Vindication of the Rights of Women* appeared in the same year as Carey's *Enquiry* and interestingly they had a common publisher and bookseller in Joseph Johnson, a nonconformist and holder of radical political views. While Paine and Wollstonecraft were writing about and engaged in radical political causes, popular protests, independence for nations and the rights of women, Carey was silent and did not raise his voice against colonial expansion or the evils of imperialism. Dharmaraj, who has studied the interrelation between colonialism and mission, concludes:

> In spite of Carey's lofty social and moral ideals in delivering the innocent victims from cruel religious practices, Carey had miserably failed from raising his voice against European political and economic oppression in India. His fight against Hindu social and

religious evils had evangelistic and missionizing goals. Carey's unwillingness to speak against the political and economic evils of the colonial government had missional and monetary aims (Dharmaraj 1993: 53).

From a postcolonial perspective it would be difficult to sustain the missionary import of Matthaean and Lukan texts which were made to serve the political and commercial interests of the West. The foregoing rereading contests both the textual features of these and past interpretative practices. It invites a reorientation in both our missiological assumptions and our exegetical conclusions. At a time when there are widespread virulent forms of religious fanaticism, a discourse with an intense missionary thrust and proselytizing tendencies will not only add confusion to an already bewildering situation, but will be difficult to sustain.

Moving beyond the Mediterranean Milieu

In my introductory remarks on postcolonialism, I referred to the liberative possibilities of contrapuntal reading in the biblical field. A further postcolonial exercise is to reclaim the New Testament writings, re-establishing them as bearers of conceptual aspects of Eastern literature. The tendency of biblical scholars to impose Christianity as the interpretative template has often blurred their vision. They have successfully promoted the belief that the New Testament writings were the product exclusively of Hellenistic and Hebraic thinking. When looking at the New Testament period and the literary productions which emerged at that time, biblical scholars maintain a deep-seated Eurocentric bias, asserting that anything theologically worthwhile can only be supplied by Greco-Judaeo traditions. In other words, Greece provides the intellectual and philosophical roots, and the Judaic heritage furnishes the religious base. In thus failing to widen their hermeneutical base, these scholars also invent a Christianity successfully insulated from any contact with Indic religions. Biblical scholars ignore the possible presence, impact and contribution of Eastern religions in the Mediterranean region during the time when the Christian faith emerged. G.B. Caird sums up the position: 'I should have thought that the Indian notion of NT dependence on Buddhism was due simply to a deficient historical sense. I certainly know of no NT scholar outside India who would give such an idea credence for a minute.'[6] But the Christian faith grew up in a cultural and literary milieu which was indeed influenced by Indian, Buddhist and Hindu thought patterns. The trade links between India and the Mediterranean Roman Empire were busier than has often been credited. Along with merchandise, religious ideas travelled both to and from the Mediterranean world. The edicts of the Emperor Asoka inform us of the presence of Buddhist missionaries in Western Asia (thirteenth edict c. 256 BCE). Theravada Buddhist monks had long been active in Alexandria before the birth of Christianity. Another, named Zarmanochegas, was sent by King Porus to Rome in 37 BCE as a member of the Indian political mission. At Athens he performed the religious act of voluntary self-immolation, and a monument was erected there in his memory. Paul, in his epistle to the Corinthians, refers to voluntarily burning himself to death: 'If I give away all I have, and if I deliver my body to be burned, but have not love, I gain nothing.'[7] Puzzled at this verse, Western Christian exegetes try to find a Judaic background, however tenuous; or they dismiss or deny that the Athens monument to the Buddhist could have had any influence on Paul (for instance, see Barrett 1960: 302-303; Bruce 1971: 125-26 and Thrall 1965: 93).

The Indian presence in the Mediterranean world, especially during the formative years of Christianity, and the possible percolation, especially of Buddhist ideas into Christian thinking, were widely acknowledged by earlier Indologists and those from the History of Religions School. The interest slackened after the First World War. One reason for this was the pressure exerted by the Vatican. Henri de Lubac was one who was silenced and reprimanded by Rome for his advocacy of Buddhist influence on Christianity.

Building on earlier comparative studies, three recent works have once again demonstrated the textual and conceptual affinities between Buddhist writings and the Gospels. Interestingly, these studies were not undertaken by biblical scholars but by historians of religion and an English literary critic. There are

6.   Quoted in Derrett (1967: 34).
7.   I owe this point to Mackenzie (1928: 41).

so many teachings and stories about Buddha and Jesus which are remarkably similar. So, too, are the ethical teachings of the two leaders, on non-violence and purity of mind. Even before the study of Q became fashionable in biblical circles, R.C. Amore argued that the Q source or the Sayings Gospel used by the first three Gospel writers, might well have been a Buddhist text. He reckons that the Gospel writers, drawing on both Jewish and Buddhist traditions, could well have refashioned them to suit the contextual needs of their time. He writes:

> There are several indications that Luke and Matthew were drawing upon a source or sources that in addition to sayings about the end of the era also contained sayings that were in effect Jewish-Christian versions of Buddhist teachings. The Sermon on the Mount has the highest concentration of these Buddhist sayings, but they are also found in quantity in later chapters of Luke and Matthew (1978: 178).

Later he goes on:

> The doctrines of the preexistence of Jesus, the stories about his birth and infancy, and the belief in his return to heaven followed the Buddhist model. This avatar pattern was combined with other interpretations of Jesus derived from Jewish expectations... I suggest that the Buddhist avatar model helped Christianity transform the Jewish messiah concept into a saviour figure that was understandable to the gentiles. Among the non-jews of the West it enabled Christianity to compete successfully with the old Hellenistic and Roman cults as well as with the old Mithra religion of the Roman Empire. Among the non-Jews of the East it enabled Christianity to supplant old Iranian religions and ironically, block the rapid westward expansion of Buddhism itself (1978: 185, 186).

The provenance of Matthew has been a vexing problem among biblical scholars. There have been proposals which locate the origin of the Gospel variously in such disparate places as Antioch and the coastal towns of Phoenician Syria. Robert Osborne, scrutinizing the special M materials in the Gospel, offers the suggestion that Edessa could be the place for the origination of Matthew's Gospel. The conceptual nature of the material in M leads Osborne to postulate eastern influence. Since Edessa was strategically placed on the famous Silk Route that linked East and West, it is possible that M materials could have been influenced by Mithraism, Zoroastrianism and Buddhism. Examining five of the

six sayings (omitting the one on divorce) in Mt. 5.21-48, which all
begin with 'You have heard that it was said...but I say to you',
Osborne detects striking parallels between these and the teaching
of Buddhism:

> These rules represent the arterial directions in which Buddhist self-
> control is to be exercised. Jesus' teaching 'on murder' (Mt. 5.21-
> 26), 'on adultery' (Mt. 5.27-30), 'on swearing' (Mt. 5.33-37), and
> 'on retaliation' (Mt. 5.38-42), to use customary headings, are
> closely paralleled in Buddha's prohibitions 'on anger, lusts of the
> flesh, untruthfulness and desire for material possessions'. More-
> over the essential spirit of each places great emphasis on the
> inward intention (1973–74: 224).

He also finds echoes of Buddhist teachings in Mt. 5.29 and 11.28-
30 and draws out the similarity between Peter walking on the
water and Buddha's disciple Sariputta attempting the same.

Moving on from the Synoptics and focusing on the Johannine
writings, Edgar Bruns is of the opinion that 'Johannine thought is
structurally closer to that of Madhymika Buddhism than it is to
either Judaic or Hellenistic thought' (1971: vii). He also postu-
lates a theory that the beloved disciple in John's Gospel could
have been modelled on the Buddhist tradition. Ananda, the
disciple of Buddha, could have been the counterpart for John.
Though there were other master–disciple relationships (Plato–
Socrates, Moses–Joshua, Elijah–Elisha, Jeremiah–Baruch), they
were faithful secretaries or in some cases authentic successors, but
'none of these were guarantors of a religious message' (1973–74:
237).

More recently, marshalling current literary methods such as
deconstruction, Zacharias Thundy has demonstrated that materials from other cultures have provided ingredients for the Gospel
narratives. In his view, many Indian stories were woven into the
Gospel texts and contemporary apocryphal literature. He has
shown that a number of stories about the childhood of Jesus cor-
respond in many details with those about the Buddha. Thundy
has also demonstrated that the Buddhist scriptural texts and traditions are older than the comparable Christian writings. Borrow-
ings, in the majority of cases, were from the East to the West. He
comes to the conclusion that non-Jewish traditions provided the
sources for stories about Jesus' childhood. In pointing out the

intertextual nature of the New Testament and Buddhist writings, he concludes that there is a 'concealed presence' of Indian ideas and motifs in the Gospel tradition:

> I add(ed) my voice to this growing critical chorus to proclaim that the New Testament is not Western literature, pure and simple, but rather still very much Eastern. This is not because the gospels were composed in the East by Orientals but because they were extensively influenced by their Oriental sources of which India and its religions were an integral part (1993: 272).

Such an acknowledgment and appropriation will enable us to go beyond the traditionally exclusive missionary claims regarding the Christian story. More importantly, it will celebrate the hybridized and eclectic nature of religious stories. It will refuse to be limited by religionist and preservationist imperatives, and ascribe fluidity to the texts.

Cautionary Markers

In conclusion, I would like to raise some of the questions that keep coming up as we engage in postcolonial discourse. My purpose is to bring some clarification into our thinking and practice. Postcolonialism may be a trendy substitute for what is known as Third World Theologies, and a convenient label for lumping together all Asian, African, Latin American, Caribbean and Pacific theologies. The caution that the Indian critic, Satchidanandan, raised in another context is equally valid for us. It could become 'another fashion in the international methodological market', or another 'new tool shaped in the West's critical foundry'. He also goes on to warn that 'postcolonialism can be neocolonialism with or without a hyphen, the empire assigning a role to former colonies and commanding them once again to speak its language' (1996: 6).

We need to pay attention to the fact that over the years the Master himself has changed, and, along with him, his language of discourse, too, has changed. The master discourse no more talks about civilizing mission. At a time when market forces are sweeping across the world in the form of globalization, the new lexicon is not about rescuing the benighted natives but concerns the universal ethics of human rights. In our discursive resistance, we tend to take a high moral ground. We employ the language of moralism, and use in our vocabularies words such as truth, responsibility, guilt, which we acquired mainly through mission and convent-school education. Hence our preoccupation with grand theorizing about how Europe underdeveloped Asia or Africa. The West we are addressing now is not familiar with such a vocabulary. Recently, through its postmodernist culture, the West has been telling us that the language of guilt, truth and responsibility are foreign to present-day multinational capitalists, international power brokers, transnational bankers and military strategists. They speak a different language—the language of success, efficiency, performance and profit. The moral agenda has moved on. Failure to note this moral shift may mean, according to Denis Ekpo, that we are barking up the wrong tree: 'We may be thinking that we are still striking at the West when in fact we may be boxing a straw West entirely of our making' (1996: 12).

The other question we need to address is whether in our writings we, the native orientalists, are replicating orientalist tendencies. Like Ali Behdad, I, too, am haunted by the question whether I am a postcolonial orientalist perpetuating the European representations of the orient within the space provided by the academy. In foregrounding the colonial constructions of the past, we may evade any discussion of the place of a postcolonial critic within the academy, and of the way we have been implicated in its power relations. As Ali Behdad says, no critic is outside the power relations of the academy, and we need to 'inquire into the implications of our critical predicaments' (1994: 138).

Postcolonialism may give the impression that the sole preoccupation of the colonized after territorial independence is colonialism. There are grave ramifications in such a postulation. Excessive interest in colonialism can cause us to ignore our histories before colonialism, and also conveniently to overlook indigenous annexations and annihilations of our people and their history. Although postcolonialism is an important political and cultural agenda, we have other equally important issues to grapple with, such as poverty, nationalism, communalism, casteism, patriarchy, internal exiles, all of which may or may not be linked to colonialism. In our eagerness to produce a resistance theory, we may ignore the minorities within our societies—dalits, women, tribals and

Burakumin. Conferring subaltern status on all these who are under-represented in our countries, we may have fallen victim to the very colonizing tendencies we seem to resist. Said warned long ago of the 'dangers and temptations…to formerly colonized peoples…of employing this structure upon themselves or upon others' (1985: 25).

Ultimately, the question is not about what to do with the hapless hyphen, or whether our project is seen as colonial or postcolonial, modern or postmodern. When we come to decide the questions that affect our communities and our people, such as, housing, health care, social security, education, homeland, the relevant questions will be about how they affect the lives of the people, rather than whether the proposal is modern or non-modern, colonial or anti-colonial. The task of postcolonialism is to ensure that the yearnings of the poor take precedence over the interests of the affluent; that the emancipation of the subjugated has primacy over the freedom of the powerful; and that the participation of the marginalized takes priority over the perpetuation of a system which systematically excludes them.

A postcolonial critic's role is not simply limited to textual dealings or literary concerns. Postcolonial hermeneutics has to be a pragmatic engagement, an engagement in which praxis is not an extra option or a subsidiary enterprise taken on in the aftermath of judicious deconstruction and reconstruction of the texts. Rather, this praxiological involvement is there from the outset of the hermeneutical process, informing and contesting the whole procedure. If we neglect this, we may become ridiculous figures like the Lavatri Alltheorie portrayed in Rukun Advani's novel, *Beethoven among the Cows*. In the longest chapter of the book entitled, 'S/he, or A Postmodern Chapter on Gender and Identity', Lavatri Alltheorie is described as a 'Post-modern theoretician, boa deconstructor, discourse analyst, post-structuralist critic, feminist historian of subalternity, colonialism and gender' (1995: 145-46). A diasporic Indian academic, she offers courses to packed audiences of white students on 'the semiology of Deconstruction and the Deconstruction of semiology' (1995: 146). The danger is that we will be seen as deliberately using catchphrases and buzzwords as a form of posture and power play. As Arun Mukherjee says, it is not enough to fight the colonizer with the 'textual weapons of irony and parody' (1996: 19). If we do so, we may, like Lavatri Alltheorie, become renowned for 'specialization in Complete Bunkum' (Advani 1995: 165).

BIBLIOGRAPHY

Advani, Rukun
    1995   *Beethoven among the Cows* (Delhi: Ravi Dayal Publisher).
Allen, Roland
    1912   *Missionary Methods: St Paul's or Ours. A Study of the Church in the Four
                Provinces* (London: Robert Scott).
Amore, Roy C.
    1978   *Two Masters, One Message: The Life and Teachings of Gautama and Jesus*
                (Nashville: Abingdon Press).
Barrett, C.K.
    1968   *A Commentary on the First Epistle to the Corinthians* (London: A. & C.
                Black).
Behdad, Ali
    1994   *Belated Travels: Orientalism in the Age of Colonial Dissolution* (Cork:
                Cork University Press).
Bhabha, Homi K.
    1994   *The Location of Culture* (London: Routledge & Kegan Paul).
Boer, Harry R.
    1961   *Pentecost and Missions* (Grand Rapids: Eerdmans).
Bosch, David J.
    1991   *Transforming Mission: Paradigm Shifts in Theology of Mission*
                (Maryknoll, NY: Orbis Books).
Bruce, F.F.
    1971   *1 and 2 Corinthians* (London: Oliphants).
Bruns, Edgar J.
    1971   *The Christian Buddhism of St John: New Insights into the Fourth Gospel*
                (New York: Paulist Press).
    1973–74   'Ananda: The Fourth Evangelist's Model for "the disciple whom
                Jesus loved" ', *Studies in Religion* 3 (3): 236-43.
Carey, William
    1961 [1792] *An Enquiry into the Obligations of Christians to Use Means for the Conver-
                sion of the Heathen* (facsimile edn with an introduction; London: The
                Carey Kingsgate Press).
Chandra, Vikram,
    1995   *Red Earth and Pouring Rain* (London: Faber & Faber).
Derrett, J. Duncan M.
    1967   'Greece and India: The Milindapanha, the Alexander Romance and
                the Gospels', *ZRGG* 19: 32-64.
Dharmaraj, Jacob S.
    1993   *Colonialism and Mission: Postcolonial Reflections* (Delhi: ISPCK).

Ekpo, Denis
    1996   'How Africa Misunderstood the West: The Failure of Anti-Western Radicalism and Postmodernity', *Third Text: Third World Perspectives on Contemporary Art and Culture* 35: 3-13.

England, John
    1996   *The Hidden History of Christianity in Asia: The Churches of the East before the year 1500* (Delhi: ISPCK).

Ferro, Marc
    1997   *Colonization: A Global History* (London: Routledge & Kegan Paul).

Kreider, Alan
    1994   'Worship and Evangelism in Pre-Christendom' (The Laing Lecture 1994), *Vox Evangelica* 24: 7-38.

Mackenzie, Donald A.
    1928   *Buddhism in Pre-Christian Britain* (London: Blakie & Sons).

Mehrez, Samia
    1991   'The Subversive Poetics of Racial Bilingualism: Postcolonial Francophone North African Literature', in Dominick LaCapra (ed.), *The Bounds of Race: Perspectives on Hegemony and Resistance* (Ithaca, NY: Cornell University Press): 255-77.

Moulton, Harold K.
    1957   *The Acts of the Apostles: Introduction and Commentary* (Madras: The Christian Literature Society).

Mukherjee, Arun P.
    1996   'Interrogating Post-colonialism: Some Uneasy Conjectures', in Harish Trivedi and Meenakshi Mukherjee (eds.), *Interrogating Post-Colonialism: Theory, Text and Context* (Shimla: Indian Institute of Advanced Study): 13-20.

Mukherjee, Meenakshi
    1996   'Interrogating Post-colonialism', in Trivedi and Mukherjee (eds.), *Interrogating Post-Colonialism: Theory, Text and Context*: 3-11.

Neill, Stephen
    1934   *Builders of the Indian Church: Present Problems in the Light of the Past* (London: Edinburgh House Press).

Osborne, Robert E.
    1973–74   'The Provenance of Matthew's Gospel', *Studies in Religion* 3 (3): 220-35.

Page, Jesse
    1921   *Schwartz of Tanjore* (London: SPCK).

Philip, T.V.
    1997   'The Missionary Impulse in the Early Asian Christian Tradition', *PTCA Bulletin* 10 (1): 5-14.

Said, Edward
    1985 [1978]   *Orientalism* (London: Penguin Books).
    1993   *Culture and Imperialism* (London: Chatto & Windus).

Sandgren, Ulla
    1991   *The Tamil New Testament and Bartholomaus Ziegenbalg* (Uppsala: Swedish Institute of Missionary Research).

Satchidanandan, K.
    1996   'The Post-Colonial Questions', *Indian Literature* 175: 5-6.
Sim, David C.
    1995   'The Gospel of Matthew and the Gentiles', *JSNT* 57: 19-48.
Spivak, Gayatri Chakravorty
    1988   *In Other Worlds: Essays in Cultural Politics* (London: Routledge &
                Kegan Paul).
    1990   *The Post-Colonial Critic: Interviews, Strategies, Dialogues* (London: Rout-
                ledge & Kegan Paul).
Stewart, John
    1928   *Nestorian Missionary Enterprise: The Story of a Church on Fire*
                (Edinburgh: T. & T. Clark).
Sugirtharajah, R.S.
    Forthcoming 1 *Asian Biblical Hermeneutics and Postcolonialism: Contesting the Interpreta-
                tions* (Maryknoll, NY: Orbis Books).
    Forthcoming 2 'Biblical Studies in India: From Imperialistic Scholarship to a Post-
                colonial Mode of Interpretation', in Fernando Segovia and Mary
                Ann Tolbert (eds.), *Teaching the Bible: Discourse and Politics of Biblical
                Pedagogy* (Maryknoll, NY: Orbis Books).
Sundkler, Bengt
    1965   *The World of Mission* (London: Lutterworth Press).
Thompson, H.P.
    1951   *Into All Lands: The History of the Society for the Propagation of the Gospel
                in Foreign Parts 1701–1950* (London: SPCK).
Thrall, Margaret E.
    1965   *The First and Second Letters of Paul to the Corinthians* (Cambridge:
                Cambridge University Press).
Thundy, Zacharias P.
    1993   *Buddha and Christ: Nativity Stories and Indian Traditions* (Leiden: E.J.
                Brill).
Townsend, John. T.
    1986   'Missionary Journeys in Acts and European Missionary Societies',
                ATR 68: 99-104.
Trivedi, Harish
    1996   'India and Post-colonial Discourse', in Harish Trivedi and
                Meenakshi Mukherjee (eds.), *Interrogating Post-Colonialism: Theory,
                Text and Context*: 231-47.
Walker, T.
    1919   *The Acts of the Apostles* (Madras: SPCK).
Ward, William
    1820   *A View of the History, Literature, and Methodology of the Hindoos: Includ-
                ing a Minute Description of their Manners and Customs and Translations
                from their Principal Works* (3 vols.; London: Black, Kingsbury, Parbury
                & Allen).

PART III

TEXTUAL STIRRINGS

Savior of the World but not of This World: A Post-Colonial Reading of Spatial Construction in John

MUSA W. DUBE

What was it about early Christian interpretation of space that made it seem so universal and translatable? That question is important for moral reflection on the colonial expansion of Christianity into the Americas, Australia, Africa and elsewhere (Swanson 1995: 241-63).

Introduction

As a post-colonial subject who inhabits colonial spaces constructed about me, for me, and against me, I begin this essay with scenes of my life and with quotations from two books. Some of the quotations are from a novel that has been designated a 'classic colonial text' (White 1993: 20); namely, Conrad's *Heart of Darkness*. The second set of quotations is from the *Aeneid*, an ancient epic that has been called 'the principal secular book of the Western World' (Knight 1956: 23). Since 'the Bible has exerted more cultural influence on the West than any other single document' (Castelli *et al*. 1994: 1), and since the Western Christian countries are imperialistic centers that colonized the world through cultural texts, and other violent devices of domination, reading these central canonical texts of the West along with John is in order.

The stories from my life and the quotations from secular texts will highlight the construction of colonizing lands and agents.[1]

---

1.   See Mudimbe (1988: 2). The term 'colonizing' in this paper defines those cultural texts, artifacts and structures that propound values which

They are intended to help the reader ask the following questions: Why does the Gospel of John characterize the world as dark and Jesus as its light (1.4-10; 8.12; 9.5; 12.46; 16.11)? Why does the Gospel of John characterize Jesus as the savior of the world but himself as not of the world (4.42; 8.23)? And, why does the Gospel of John say the church/Christian believers do not belong to this world, while it also sends them to the world (15.18-22; 20.21)?

Further, the quotations from secular narratives enable us to take a post-colonial interdisciplinary approach. I employ them to decolonize the exclusively divine space assigned to the biblical texts. By placing John's Gospel in synoptic parallels with *Heart of Darkness* and the *Aeneid*, my aim is to decolonize Jesus' highly exalted divinity and his place of origin insofar as they will be shown to express a colonizing ideology.[2]

The scenes from my life, on the other hand, serve as another text and another book in writing, precisely because I wish to resist focusing on canons that were given to the colonized by the empire. These extended scenes of my life may make some readers impatient, as they think, 'when will she get to the biblical text?' Let it be understood, then, that my stories are meant to contest, subvert and decolonize the master's text by refusing to give it too much attention. However slight this strategy of resistance may seem, it reflects my growing discontent with the strategy of reading the colonizer's canon. I suspect that the massive inclusive power of the empire (which seeks to keep the colonized as devotees rather than equals) may be drawing me in for its own purposes. For these reasons, I constantly problematize my very position as a biblical student, trained in Western schools, Western texts and Western ways of reading. With this introduction, I turn to the scenes from my life.

authorize the domination of space, the reformation of native minds, and the integration of local economic histories into structures of the colonizers.

2. The Gospel of John was indeed written by an oppressed minority group (9.22; 12.42; 16.2, 20, 33) and among the colonized Jews (10.47; 18.28–19.42). This setting in itself, however, does not automatically guarantee that it is an anti-imperial text. Post-colonial studies indicate that the colonized do not always resist their oppressors: they also collaborate and imitate the imperial power at various stages of their oppression.

Scene One

The plane is landing and I peer outside. It is grey, dull, rainy and gloomy. My neighborly British passenger says, 'Welcome to England. It is one of our beautiful days.' I take a train from Kings Cross and travel north to Durham. I am struck that Great Britain is so little. I arrive in my college and I am the only black student. Unknowingly, I continue to dress according to the desert dictates of my country: I change my clothes every other day and soon a myth begins that I am an African princess. When Christmas comes I receive at least ten invitations to join families for the season. I decide to visit a number of families. Each time I arrive in a new home they say, 'Where is Botswana?' And so an atlas is brought out and consulted, and every time, there is no Botswana on the map. It is Bechuanaland. My hosts apologize and promise to buy a new atlas.

Evidently, my journey from the so-called 'Dark Continent' into the heart of the empire indicates that lands or physical bodies are ideological constructs. It highlights the lack of direct relationship between the depiction of certain lands and their physical features. For example, I kept thinking that Britain should be the heart of darkness, given that it is so gloomy, that its people hardly smile and that its sun hardly ever goes across the wide sky. I wondered why I had heard that Britain was a place where the sun never sets, when its sun hardly goes across God's wide skies. Indeed, I found it difficult to understand why little Britain was called Great Britain, for it made more sense to describe it as a little island. These apparent contradictions, however, did not stop me from saying Britain was like 'heaven', when a British friend asked me what I thought of Britain. The moment I pronounced it 'heaven', I became aware that most of the pictures of heaven which I had innocently consumed in Sunday school lessons were based on Western landscapes.

Scene Two

I inform Aluta, my nine-year-old son, that we will be visiting a new church tomorrow. He sits up and says to me, 'Mama, please, do not tell them that we are from Africa.' In another incident, I inform him that we will be going for a weekend retreat with some American families, and he says to me, 'Mama, please, do not tell them that we are from Africa.'

'Why?' I ask. 'Cuz when I tell people that I am from Africa, they laugh, they make fun of me, and say we eat boars.' 'Well, tell them that you are from Botswana,' I say to him. 'What's the difference?' he says, 'Botswana is in Africa.' 'Botswana is not Africa,' I say. 'I will go if you promise not to say we are from Africa.' 'Do you want me to lie?' I ask. 'No, Mama. You do not have to lie. Tell them we are African Americans.' We reach a deal that I will not tell, although we do not discuss the people who ask. The moment our American friends arrive, they begin to discuss The Gods Must Be Crazy, Out of Africa, Tarzan, *and some other Western movies produced about Africa. I see my son's eyebrows rising in suppressed panic, and I smile silently and reassuringly back to him.*

Basically, Aluta discovers that he bears upon his little body the map of a strange, darkened Africa—an Africa he never knew prior to his coming to North America—and he does not like it. The dark shadow of Western maps of Africa, however, looms high above him, following him through the books, the big screen, the TV and through the conversations he holds. My son resists the North American maps of Africa that are imposed upon him. He would rather be an African American. He would rather come from a different map, a different place, a better world, in his view, North America. Among other things, his response demonstrates that people redraw or change their designated spaces for the purposes of power—including claiming the same space as their oppressor. Similarly, John's redrawing of spatial maps will be shown to be a quest for power by an oppressed group, which seeks power on the same terms (ideology) as its imperial oppressors and their collaborators.

As a subject who largely occupies the darkened spaces of Africa, I have thus come to be keenly suspicious of the authors of maps, and to interrogate their motivation for calling certain 'little' places 'great' or certain gloomy and dark places lands of continuous light and vice versa. These disparities make me realize that maps are not neutral, stable or fixed. Rather, they are 'spaces' that are subject to manipulation. My question, therefore, is, what is the purpose of depicting the colonizing lands in terms that explode their physical features, and how is that related to the negative spatial depiction of colonized lands? These invented and contradictory stories, of course, highlight the rhetoric of space, subject and power. I now turn to highlight the narrative designs of colonizing maps and agents from a contemporary novel and an ancient epic.

Writing Imperial Spaces and Subjects

In *Heart of Darkness*, Mr Kurtz, the protagonist and master colonizer who was supposedly the product of 'all Europe' (Conrad 1981: 83) has to be forcefully removed from Africa. In the scene of his capture the narrator describes him as follows: 'He looked at least seven feet long...I saw him open his mouth wide...as *though he had wanted to swallow all the air, all the earth, all the men before him'* (Conrad 1981: 101, emphasis mine). The narrator says,

> I had...to invoke him—himself—his own exalted and incredible degradation. *There was nothing either above or below him, and I knew it. He had kicked himself loose of the very earth.* Confound the man! He had kicked the very earth to pieces. He was alone, and I before him did not know whether I stood on the ground or floated in the air. (Conrad 1981: 112).

And, Mr Kurtz's 'stare...was wide enough to embrace the whole universe, piercing enough to penetrate all the hearts that beat in the darkness' (1981: 119).

The *Aeneid* is an epic that was written to mythologize the rise of the Roman Empire. The following quotation is from a scene where Aeneas's ships had been wrecked on the coast of Africa at Carthage. In this disaster, Aeneas, the destined founder of the Roman Empire, is reassured of his position in the following words:

> The creator of gods and human kind smiled...and then spoke ...'You shall exalt to the stars of Heaven your son Aeneas... *To Romans I set no boundary in space or time.* I have granted them dominion, and it has no end... I will foster the nation which wears the toga, the Roman nation, masters of the world. My decree is made (Virgil, *Aeneid* 1. 257-82).

These quotations indicate three factors central to the construction of space, subjects and colonialism. First, colonizing subjects and their races, exemplified by Mr Kurtz and Aeneas, are described as larger than life. Kurtz, was supposedly seven feet tall, and his humanity borders on divinity since, he was 'exalted' and had to be 'invoked'.[3] Second, Mr Kurtz's exalted status is notably described in relation to space: he had 'kicked himself loose of the very earth', 'he had kicked the very earth to pieces', to the extent that 'there was nothing above or below him!' The power to kick free of the earth, the power to have nothing below or above someone, graphically illustrates the art of drawing colonizing maps. The colonizer is above the limitation of boundaries. Yet the nineteenth- to twentieth-century colonizer represented by Mr Kurtz and acting out his artistry in the heart of Africa is only described as free of the earth primarily to legitimize his claim over the whole of Africa, and all other non-European places. To use the narrator's words, Mr Kurtz has kicked himself free from the earth precisely because he wants to 'swallow...all the earth'.

The *Aeneid* reflects a similar pattern of constructing colonizing agents as divine and in relation to physical space. First, Aeneas is reportedly exalted 'to the stars of Heaven'. This description places him above ordinary human beings and ranks him among divine beings. Second, as the chosen founder of the Roman Empire, Aeneas's greatness, and, by extension that of his race, is notably described in relation to the physical spaces of the earth: The creator of Gods declares that '*To Romans, I set no boundary in space or time!*' The Romans are declared the '*masters of the world*'. Once again, the description designates them above earthly spaces in order to legitimate their possession of this world.

The imperial settings of these quotations are centuries apart, yet we see in both the art of drawing colonizing maps and agents: colonizing agents and their races befriend divinity and imagine all spaces of the earth to be universally available to them. These legitimizing narratives present the projects of colonization as acceptable by constructing the colonizing subjects as larger than life, divine, and bearing passports to every corner of the earth. The world lies at their feet.

This brings me to a post-colonial reading of John's construction of space.[4] In the light of the construction of colonizing maps and

3. Conrad 1981: 115-19; Mr Kurtz's divinity is quite elaborate since he is characterized as the 'Voice', and at his death, the narrator says, 'it was as though a veil had rent'. This description evokes the death of Jesus.

4. The Gospel of John is a post-colonial narrative since it was born within the Roman Empire and from a colonized race. The imperial setting is

agents, elaborated above, what is the ideological function of characterizing Jesus as savior of the world while denying that he is of
this world?[5] To highlight the power rhetoric at work, I will focus
on a few aspects of the spatial construction and Jesus' origins in
the prologue (1.1-18) and ch. 3, and how it conveys colonizing
values.

In the Beginning

One of the striking features of John is its opening. The book
begins not on this earth, not in any known human places, not in
the time of this world. The book begins 'in the beginning'. What
is the function of this outer space? Why does John construct a spatial setting that disavows earthly spaces? Is it because John wishes
to disassociate Jesus and his followers/believers/readers from the
world?

As will be shown, this planting of the narrative in outer space
precisely serves to lay a claim on this world. Like Mr Kurtz, who
had kicked himself loose of this very earth and who had nothing
above or below him, or like Aeneas who was exalted to the 'stars
of Heaven', this construction of space is heavily invested in claiming power over all places in the world and its various peoples. It
serves to authorize certain agents with unlimited powers over the
world. Accordingly, the ideological function of the 'in the beginning' spatial setting is evident in the first four verses, which read
as follows:

> In the beginning was the Word, and the Word was with God, and
> the Word was God. He was in the beginning with God. All things
> came into being through him, and without him not one thing
> came into being. In him was life, and the life was the light of all the
> people.

'The beginning' is the place and time where the Word was, and
where the Word virtually created all things that were created. The
Word, who is later identified as Jesus (1.29) is not only elevated to

evident particularly in the arrest and death of Jesus (11.48; 19.12).

5.   See Neyrey (1988: 94-111) for an exploration of 'Equal to God, but
not of this world'. Neyrey regards it as an 'ideology of revolt' against flesh or
material things that was not only sparked by conflict with the larger Jewish
society, but also by internal divisions within the Johannine community.

pre-existent time and place (see also 8.58; 17.5, 24), he was living with God. Moreover, 'the Word was God' (see also 5.19-20; 10.30; 20.28). This startling phrase, like the whole Gospel, presents Jesus and God as almost inseparable and equal (8.58; 20.28). As the creator of all things, Jesus is the source of life, for 'without him not one thing came into being'.

'The beginning', therefore, describes the origin of Jesus as outside this world. 'In the beginning' is where Jesus lived with God, who is also identified as his Father (1.18). In the beginning is where Jesus came from. The importance of constructing Jesus' original space in these terms pertains to two factors: first, the power of the Father God who lives is in the beginning; second, the 'spaceless space' of the Father gives Jesus power over the world since Jesus originates from the beginning of the world as the creator of the world, and, since 'no-one' else has ever seen the Father except the Son who has made him known (1.18).

No One Has Ever Seen God

'In the beginning' as a spatial construction also serves to legitimate a systematic subordination of all other individuals or groups that occupy the spaces of this world (except, of course, Jesus' followers). Accordingly, the Gospel of John engages in a long and extended subordination of all other Jewish figures and the cultural spaces of power associated with them.[6] It begins in the prologue with John the Baptist who, we are told, 'came to testify to the light', but 'he himself was not the light' (vv. 7-8),[7] the true light being, of course, Jesus Christ (v. 9). In the closing verses of the prologue (17-18), Moses is acknowledged as bringer of the Law, while grace and truth come through Jesus Christ. The revelatory roles of Moses and Jesus are immediately followed by a disclaimer stating that 'no-one has ever seen God', except for God's

6. Among many others who have studied this phenomenon, see Peterson (1993), for a comprehensive analysis of the whole Gospel of John.

7. Peterson (1993: 109-32) highlights that the characterization of Jesus as the 'Word' is a subordination of Sophia, since Jesus assumes her position and role; moreover, he becomes superior to her, for he was from the beginning with God and almost indistinguishable from God. Also, while Sophia became the Law, Jesus brought grace and truth.

only son, who is close to the Father's heart, who has made him known' (v. 18; see also 6.46).

This systematic subordination is emphatically repeated throughout the Gospel of John with different figures. For example, ch. 3 recalls John the Baptist and Moses again, with another figure of authority, Nicodemus, all of them representing particular interest groups in Jewish society.

He Who Comes from Above is Above All

To begin with Nicodemus, he is identified as a 'leader of the Jews' (3.1) and a 'teacher of Israel' (3.10).[8] The narrative techniques for subjugating Nicodemus to Jesus include that 'he came to Jesus' (3.2) and that Nicodemus declares Jesus 'a teacher from God' (3.2). Jesus seizes upon Nicodemus's inquiry to declare and claim that 'No-one can see the kingdom of God without being born from above' (3.3, 7). These two verses combine 'no-one' with 'from above' to subordinate Nicodemus, who is not born 'from above'. By extension, it subordinates all the teachers and leaders of Israel and their followers to the high authority of Jesus and his disciples.

Nicodemus' social position is further discredited through characterizing him as ignorant and elevating Jesus as knowledgeable on the basis of his origins: Jesus asks Nicodemus, 'You are a teacher of Israel, and yet you do not understand these things?' Then Jesus says, 'we speak of what we know and testify what we have seen' (3.11). As v. 13 clarifies, the testimony of Jesus and his followers is trustworthy because, '*no-one* has ascended into heaven except the one who descended from heaven, the Son of Man' (emphasis mine). The followers of Jesus speak of what they 'know' and have 'seen', precisely because Jesus is the only one who has seen and knows the Father.

As in the prologue (1.17-18), Moses is recalled again, acknowledged and surpassed (3.13-15) for while Moses lifted a lifeless snake to save life in the 'wilderness', Jesus who descended 'from heaven' will be lifted up himself, not to give just life, but 'eternal life' (see also 6.32-51; 7.19-24). Moses, who is a historical and

---

8.   For a more detailed study of Nicodemus see Meeks (1972), and Rensberger (1988: 37-63).

significant cultural figure in the history of the Jewish people, is thus coopted into accentuating the importance of Jesus. Moses is subordinated even in his power over his own followers, the arch-rivals of the disciples of Jesus (9.28-31).

The narrative swiftly moves over to John the Baptist. It adopts a textual strategy of subordinating the authority of John the Baptist to Jesus. In a classic narrative design, John the Baptist proclaims his own subordination: Jesus 'must increase, but I must decrease' (3.30). Jesus' elevation is once again grounded in his origins as John the Baptist announces that 'no-one can receive anything except what was given from heaven' (3.27). John the Baptist proclaims the greatness of Jesus, holding that

> The one who comes from above is above all; the one who is of the earth belongs to the earth and speaks about earthly things. The one who comes from heaven is above all. He testifies to what he has seen and heard... The Father loves the Son and places all things in his hands (3.31-32, 35).

As many scholars note, the authority of Jesus is emphatically heightened over all other cultural figures of note and their earthly spaces of authority, through constructing the spatial origins of Jesus as 'from above', 'from heaven', and by emphasizing that 'no-one' has ever 'seen' or 'heard' God except for Jesus who descended from the Father/Heaven. The function of an out-of-this-world spatial origin, however, is precisely to take control of this world. This is evident in John the Baptist's repeated assertions that 'one who comes from above is above all', that the 'one who comes from heaven is above all', and that the 'Father...places all things in his hands'. This is power over earthly powers rather than other heavenly beings.

One cannot overemphasize the repetitiveness of John's Gospel and its focused intention of highlighting the superiority of Jesus through constructing the highest and most unique place of origin. Each time that a rhetorical question is asked, such as, 'Are you greater than our ancestor Jacob?' (4.12),[9] or, 'Are you greater than Abraham our Father who died?' (8.53), the answer is always affirmative. Jesus' superiority is always based on his origins; thus,

---

9. See Neyrey (1979), for the ideology of recalling Jacob in the story of the Samaritan woman.

he gives superior water and bread that, unlike that given by the ancestors, which people ate and died, leads to eternal life. 'The beginning', 'heaven' and 'above' are the places of power. They are spaces of the Father. Because Jesus comes from above, because he is the only one who has seen, who has heard, who knows the Father, he becomes the truth, the light, the true bread, the life, the only Son, and the only way to the Father in this world.

The struggle for power in John's text is undoubtedly between local Jewish groups (primarily the disciples of Moses and the disciples of Jesus), for, as Norman Peterson shows, they both claim allegiance to the same cultural spaces and historical subjects. Consequently, the subordination of prophets, of Sophia, Moses and Abraham proceeds first by acknowledging them, then by showing that in fact they testify to Jesus, and then elevating Jesus above them (Peterson 1993: 80-110). It is, therefore, quite tempting to locate the conflict in the Gospel as a reflection of conflict between national Jewish groups or conflict within the Johannine community itself, while overlooking a very important factor: the presence of the empire.

As a post-colonial reader, my study of these local conflicts is a study of the impact of colonialism and the response of the colonized—those whose cultural, political and social boundaries have been entered by a foreign and forceful power, which controls largely from outside. The presence of the imperial power, the Roman Empire, is the catalyst for the vicious competition of local groups. It is the small grain of yeast that leavens the whole bread, breeding conflict and competition as local groups respond by trying to redefine culture, or to provide solutions. John's very focus is 'Christology' or the 'King of the Jews', a theme that attests to the imperial context and the concerns and hopes of colonized Jewish people.

Yet, as this study partially shows, the colonized groups' response to their subjugation takes various conflicting positions at different stages of their domination. Inevitably, the response includes stages of partial acceptance of foreign domination, complete acceptance, complete rejection or revolt (all these stages often occurring at the same time, reflected in different interest groups). Moreover, the struggle for power among the colonized is not only between the colonized and the colonizer. It also involves conflict and competition among the various colonized interest groups/ political parties as they scramble to define reality within their invaded boundaries, or as they fight for the attention of their colonizer; where they have lost power (Overman 1990: 66-68). In the process of resistance, the colonized groups can also imagine themselves in power on the same terms as their oppressors. If one locates the Johannine community within the setting of the colonized, the text not only reflects conflict and competition among the local groups, it also assumes narrative designs that propound imperializing ideologies. Its strategy of elevating Jesus above any other cultural figure among the Jews and in the world, for instance, is a colonizing ideology.

'As the Father sent me, I send you' (20.21b)

The rigorous elevation of Jesus in space and time not only subordinates all other Jewish places and subjects, it claims power over the whole world. Jesus becomes the creator of the world, the savior of the world, the one who comes from the Father, and who is above all (1.3, 10; 3.31-34; 4.42). The story of the Johannine Jesus, therefore, does not end in John, or with the disciples of Jesus and Moses, who are in a vicious competition for power. Rather, it explodes the boundaries of its origins, and its immediate context, to touch and lay claim upon every part of the earth.

In the farewell discourse and the resurrection appearances we thus witness a formal transference of power and an insistence on the continuation of the Johannine Jesus story. Jesus, and the disciples or church/believers enter into a relationship that is closely modelled on the relationship of the Father and the Son. First, Jesus says his disciples or believers 'do not belong to the world' because he has 'chosen' them 'out of the world' (15.19). Second, Jesus prays to the Father saying,

> As you have sent me into the world, so I sent them into the world... As you, Father, are in me and I am in you may they also be in us, so that the world may believe that you have sent me. The glory that you have given me I have given to them, so that they may be one, as we are one (17.18, 21-22).

In one of his resurrection appearances the Johannine Jesus meets the disciples and, once more, says, 'as the Father has sent me, so I

send you' (20.21b). In other words, Christ's followers or Christian
believers do not belong to this world. They have been chosen out
of this world, yet they are sent into the world! This seemingly contradictory construction of Christian agents and their relation to
the world imitates the status of Jesus, who is a savior of this world
but who is apparently not of this world. Put differently, the transference of power to the disciples or Christian church gives them
power to travel into all other cultural worlds and spaces with the
same power and method of devaluing and subordinating differences, that characterize the Johannine Jesus.

Colonized or Colonizing Biblical Studies

Since Two-Thirds World post-colonial readers experienced Western colonization as a textual and military exercise of subjugating
difference, and since 'the Bible has exerted more cultural
influence on the West than any other single document', the question of examining the role of biblical texts in authorizing imperialism is imperative. Many Western scholars have done detailed
studies on the Johannine construction of Jesus and its origin,
yielding excellent expositions. Yet the question of John's role in
sanctioning Western imperialism is hardly ever raised. Peterson's
book *The Gospel of John and the Sociology of Light,* for instance, offers
an excellent study of John's method of subordinating other cultural spaces and subjects and elevating Jesus and his followers. Yet
Peterson constantly refers to John's method as 'anti-structural',
without acknowledging that it subordinates all other Jewish subjects, not in search of a liberating paradigm, but to install Jesus
and his followers in a position that is higher than any known
earthly place and people. Similarly, Neyrey's book *An Ideology of
Revolt* only focuses on the conflict and competition with other
colonized Jewish groups and within the Johannine community
itself. Neyrey does not ask if this 'ideology of the revolt', revolts
against the colonizing enemy, that is, the Roman Empire, or
whether John reflects conflict and competition in the face of a
central enemy.

It is important, however, to ask if John, as a post-colonial text,
focuses on other victims. If John focuses on other colonized
groups, one must further ask how John's stance came to be used

in later generations and centuries. Does the Johannine perspective serve, or has it served, as an anti-imperial or pro-imperial text? Basically, Peterson and Neyrey do not seek to understand how the response of the Johannine community to the Roman Empire, and other early church groups,[10] is related to the Bible as a text of the West, and the West as an imperialistic center. Further, their focus on the internal conflicts of the colonized, without highlighting the presence and role of colonizer, shelters the exploitation and oppressiveness of the empire on its subjects. Failure to keep the empire in view as a central player unwittingly maintains the structures of oppression in the past and the present.

Western academic biblical readings, therefore, tend to read the Johannine texts, and other books of the Bible, as if they only refer to ancient times and have nothing to do with our current world. The reluctance to cross the borderline of the ancient setting and to assess how the biblical texts, together with such texts as *Heart of Darkness* and the *Aeneid*, inform contemporary structures of power in the world (Mazrui 1990: 1-18, is one way in which biblical studies are not only colonized, but become a colonizing body of knowledge. Biblical studies vigilantly guards the boundaries, insisting on reading biblical texts without assessing or relating them to modern and contemporary world politics. For the most part biblical texts are read in isolation from other secular works of literature. Whether this is intended or not, this approach maintains and perpetuates the imperialistic power of the West over non-Western and non-Christian places, peoples and cultures.

And this is the point where my reading of John differs: it refuses to ignore the yeast of the Roman imperial setting in John's Gospel; it refuses to abstract the biblical texts from modern and contemporary international structures; it also refuses to read the biblical text in isolation from other works of literature. I therefore hold that the Johannine approach of exalting Jesus to divine status, above all Jewish figures and above all other cultural figures of the world, is a colonizing ideology that is not so different from the ideology of the *Aeneid* and *Heart of Darkness*. More importantly,

10. For example, Rom. 13.1-7 and 1 Pet. 2.13-25 suggest a sanctification of imperialism, but the apocalyptic book of Revelation reflects revolt and resistance.

John's colonizing ideology calls upon academic readers to go beyond just expounding and explaining the construction of John's text. Rather, readers are called upon to decolonize its ideology and to work on readings of liberating interdependence between Christians and Jews, One-Third World and Two-Thirds World, Western and Non-Western, Christian and Non-Christian cultures, women and men, etc.

There is a general insistence on confining academic biblical studies to ancient times among scholars, or on reading the text in isolation from modern and contemporary international structures. Nevertheless, the following are some of the reasons that call for a post-colonial reading of John and the Bible as a whole. First, it is generally acknowledged that 'the Bible has exerted more cultural influence on the West than any single document (Castelli *et al.* 1994: 1). Second, it is a fact that most of the Western Christian countries are also the imperialistic centers that colonized the world through cultural texts and other violent devices of domination (Said 1992: 12-14; Boehmer 1995: 44-59). Third, modern church history, which shows that Christian missions and other colonizing institutions and agents worked smoothly together in modern and contemporary colonialism, (Mudimbe 1988: 44-64) calls on readers to investigate the relationship of biblical ideology to contemporary international structures. Lastly, and specifically to John, mission studies indicate that John's Gospel has been the most influential text.

How and why the Bible has been such a usable text in the colonizing agendas, and how we should read it in the post-colonial era are questions that, I believe, should no longer be bracketed in academic biblical studies. Thus, I began this article with readings from my life, and two narratives to highlight the modern and ancient colonial art of drawing spaces and subjects, and its goals. My aim was to highlight the colonizing strategies and their similarity to the Gospel of John. From this perspective, the exalted space of Jesus as a savior of the world, who is not of this world, is shown to be a colonizing ideology that claims power over all other places and peoples of the earth—one which is not so different from other constructions in secular literature.

My reading thus calls for a decolonization of a number of things. First, of the overtly divine characterization of Jesus and his

place of origin in the Gospel of John. Second, since this colonizing power was transferred to Christians (sending them to this
world, while denying that they are of this world) it also necessi-
tates a decolonization of Christian claims over all other places and
religious cultures of the world. Put differently, my reading calls
for an academic biblical studies that also assesses the impact of
biblical texts on modern and contemporary international relations. Lastly, my reading not only calls for decolonization, it also
seeks a liberating interdependence of cultural differences and
economic systems.

Conclusion

As the opening quotation from Tod Swanson's article on John 4
and 6 showed, Swanson began by asking questions that related the
modern imperialism of the Christian West to the biblical text.
Swanson goes on to ask:

> Why have Christians so often thought it permissible and even
> morally imperative to carry their message across all boundaries,
> invading the homelands of other communities? (1995: 241-63)

Such questions have not informed academic biblical studies given
that academic biblical study was born in the age of modern colonialism, and remains within the imperialistic centers of the West.
In the post-colonial era, however, these questions should no
longer be bracketed. Post-colonial readings of the Bible must seek
to decolonize the biblical text, its interpretations, its readers, its
institutions, as well as seeking ways of reading for liberating interdependence. Liberating interdependence here entails a twofold
willingness on the part of readers: first, to propound biblical readings that decolonize imperialistic tendencies and other oppressive
narrative designs; second, to propound readings that seek to highlight the biblical texts and Jesus as undoubtedly important
cultures, which are, nonetheless, not 'above all' but among the
many important cultures of the world.

BIBLIOGRAPHY

Bammer, Angelika (ed.)
1994 *Displacements: Cultural Identities in Question* (Bloomington: Indiana
University Press).

Blaut, J.M.
1993   *The Colonizer's Model of the World: Geographical Diffusionism and Euro-centric History* (New York: Guildford Press).

Blunt, Alison, and Gillian Rose
1994   *Writing Women and Space: Colonial and Post-colonial Geographies* (New York: Guildford Press).

Boehmer, Elleke
1995   *Colonial and Post-colonial Literature* (New York: Oxford University Press).

Brueggemann, Walter
1994   'Exodus', in *The New Interpreter's Bible: A Commentary* (Nashville: Abingdon Press).

Cassidy, Richard J.
1992   *John's Gospel in New Perspective* (New York: Orbis Books).

Castelli, Elizabeth *et al.* (eds.)
1994   *The Postmodern Bible: The Bible and Culture Collective* (New Haven: Yale University Press).

Conrad, Joseph
1981   *Heart of Darkness and the Secret Sharer* (New York: Bantam Classics [1902]).

Donaldson, Laura E.
1993   *Decolonizing Feminisms: Race Gender and Empire Building* (Chapel Hill: University of North Carolina Press).

Kirby, Kathleen M.
1996   *Indifferent Boundaries: Spatial Concepts of Human Subjectivity* (New York: Guildford Press).

Knight, Jackson, W.F. (trans.)
1956   *Virgil: The Aeneid* (Harmondsworth: Penguin Books).

Koester, Craig
1990   'The Savior of the World (John 4:42)', *JBL* 109: 665-80.

Kysar, Robert
1976   *John: The Maverick Gospel* (Louisville: John Knox Press).

Martyn, J.L.
1978   *History and Theology in the Gospel of John* (Nashville: Abingdon Press).

Mazrui, Ali
1990   *Cultural Forces in World Politics* (London: James Curry).

Meeks, Wayne
1972   'A Man from Heaven in Johannine Sectarianism', *JBL* 91: 44-72.

Mohanty, Chandra T.
1991   'Cartographies of Struggle: Third World Women and the Politics of Feminism', in C.T. Mohanty, Ann Russo and Lourdes Torres (eds.), *Third World Women and the Politics of Feminism* (Bloomington: Indiana University Press): 1-47.

Mudimbe, V.Y.
1988   *The Invention of Africa: Gnosis, Philosophy and the Order of Knowledge* (Bloomington: Indiana University Press).

Neyrey, Jerome
    1979   'Jacob Tradition and the Interpretation of John 4.10-26', *CBQ* 41: 419-37.
    1988   *An Ideology of Revolt* (Philadelphia: Fortress Press).
Overman, Andrew
    1990   *Matthew's Gospel and Formative Judaism: The Social World of the Matthean Community* (Minneapolis: Fortress Press).
Peterson, Norman
    1993   *The Gospel of John and the Sociology of Light: Language and Characterization in the Fourth Gospel* (Valley Forge: Trinity Press International).
Quint, David
    1993   *Epic and Empire* (Princeton, NJ: Princeton University Press).
Rensberger, David
    1988   *Johannine Faith and Liberating Community* (Philadelphia: Westminster Press).
Said, Edward
    1992   *Culture and Imperialism* (New York: Alfred Knopf).
Segovia, Fernando F.
    1991   'Journey(s) of the Word: A Reading of the Plot of the Fourth Gospel', *Semeia* 53: 23-54.
Swanson, Tod
    1995   'To Prepare a Place: Johannine Christianity and the Collapse of Ethnic Territory', *JAAR* LXII (2): 241-63.
Talbert, Charles
    1994   *Reading John: A Literary and Theological Commentary on the Fourth Gospel and the Johannine Epistles* (New York: Crossroads).
White, Jonathan (ed.)
    1993   *Recasting the World: Writing after Colonialism* (Baltimore: The Johns Hopkins University Press).
Wimbush, Vincent
    1996   '...Not of This World...: Early Christianities as Rhetorical and Social Formation', in Elizabeth Castelli and Hal Taussig (eds.), *Reimagining Christian Origins: A Colloquium Honoring Burton L. Mack* (Valley Forge: Trinity Press International): 23-36.

Places at the Table:
Feminist and Postcolonial Biblical Interpretation

SHARON H. RINGE

Introduction: Colonized and Colonizers

Feminists of the dominant culture of the United States find ourselves in the ambiguous position of colonizers and colonized
people at the same time. As women, we have come under the
political and discursive colonial projects of kyriarchy (domination
of elite males over non-elite males and over women [Schüssler
Fiorenza 1994: 14]). As members of the dominant culture, we
cannot even fight our own colonized status without also participating in structures and systems that express and support the discursive and political colonial projects of Euro-American capitalism. This dilemma arises from the fact that when we struggle for
our 'rights' of access to and participation in the political, economic, educational, religious, and other social systems that prevail
in our society and world, we support those same systems in their
exclusion of others in our own society—persons of color and poor
people, for instance—and in their exploitation of groups and
entire peoples whose economic, military, or political situation
makes them dependent on decisions and strategies of the West.

The traditional way of avoiding the pain of that ambiguity has
been to ignore both aspects—to proceed as though we were both
unharmed and harmless. Thus, until recently we have ignored the
significance that our dominated status as women has for our work.
Recognizing that, however, and turning to 'advocacy scholarship'
(which had replaced the ideals and pretense to disinterested
scholarship that we had been taught) in order to overcome our
own marginalization, did not lead us immediately to recognize
our role as part of a system that dominates other people and

peoples (Spivak 1988b: 131; Trinh 1989: 85-86).

The former has proven the easier aspect of our dilemma for women interpreters of the Bible to address, as it has for feminists in other fields of inquiry. In the past several decades, women biblical interpreters have accompanied women scholars in other disciplines in the task of lifting up the stories and situations of women usually rendered invisible in social institutions, in history, in literature and in traditional scholarship. Like scholars in academic women's studies programs and in research projects outside the academy, women readers of the Bible (with or without the political commitment to feminism) have highlighted women's presence in the biblical text where we were thought to be absent, and we learned the art of listening for the silent and silenced voices, to read the history of women in the biblical worlds between the lines of official documentation and analysis of those periods (Sakenfeld 1988: 5-18). Without allowing ourselves to recognize the broader manifestation of the Western colonial project, reinforced by the textual inscription of dominant values and readings of history both within the Bible and in its dominant interpretations (Spivak 1990:1, 62), we became adept at identifying its 'patriarchal' or 'kyriarchal' manifestations, and we learned to 'graf(ph)t' (Donaldson 1992: 59-60) texts and their ancient and modern contexts to encourage the bearing of new fruit from the reading task.

That blend of perception and imperception reflects our education, which has been normed by the values of the dominant culture. In the midst of an education allegedly aimed at critical consciousness and assessment of the world, we have also been schooled in strategic non-perception of the inconsistencies between the articulated values of that culture, and the values embodied in its institutions that function 'well'—in other words, to our advantage. Whether it is a matter of this 'trained incapacity', in which the very skills we have acquired work to subvert their own best use (Burke 1984: 7), or a simple failure of nerve, the result is that many European and North American feminist biblical interpreters have shared with our sisters in other disciplines the ability to take seriously our own situation as oppressed or marginalized people without developing sophistication about other dimensions of the same colonial project.

By this failure, coupled with our new-found voice in the scholarly community and on the political agenda, we have demonstrated how well we learned our lesson from our own colonizers who, by and large, ran the institutions of the world, inscribed meaning onto the world by the history and literature they produced and codified its values into language. As we had heard ourselves subsumed under 'mankind' and rendered invisible in histories and literature that focused on men's exploits without asking about the subjective circumstances of women, children, or the rest of the ecosystem, so now we did to all 'women'. In assertions about 'woman' or 'women', and in pleas for 'sisterhood', we often posited gender as the only significant *discrimen* in human experience. Our perspective led to insights about the role of women in—or absent from—biblical texts, and about the consequences of traditional or otherwise authoritative readings of those texts for women's lives. We affirmed that to introduce the pronoun 'she' is not just to change a word, and 'woman's voice is not one voice to be added to the orchestra' (Spivak 1988b: 132). Instead, that addition introduces the question of gender as a heuristic category that changes the shape of the entire analysis of the literature or portrayal of history.

Really, though, with this apparently open and courageous rhetoric, we were talking about women like us (Donaldson 1992: 1). Our concern was how *we* would participate in the benefits of the economy, society and culture conveyed and given a blessing in the literature, and to which our ethnic, racial and class identity 'should' give us access. But we conveniently overlooked the differences created by those other categories of our identity, and generalized from our experience into a romantic caricature of Everywoman (Spivak 1988a: 82). We ignored race, culture, class, marital status, sexual orientation, and a host of other factors that shape women's lives, make them different from one another, and result in specific manifestations of oppression and exclusion in the 'multiply organized' lives of women outside the dominant culture (Lionnet 1995: 5-6). As a consequence, our work generalized from our own experience in a renewed silencing and objectifying of such categories of women as women of color, poor women, lesbians, and women from other parts of the world (Mohanty 1984: 259-63).

A first step taken along the path toward recognizing the diversity of women's voices needs to be highlighted because of its dangerous seductiveness. That step has been the condescending effort of women academics of the dominant culture to 'represent' in the sense of speaking for other groups of women whom we do not 'represent' in the sense of coming from their culture or community (Spivak 1988a: 70). The violence done to those women as subjects engaged in naming and articulating their worlds is twofold. In the first place, the pretense of our speaking for 'them' implies that they have not always been speaking for themselves, simply because their language of discourse has been different from our own. They are erased as subjects to whose truth claims others must pay attention, and reduced to the grammatical objects of others' discourse, including now the discourse of other women (Hutcheon 1989: 130-35). (Indeed, the danger of falling into that trap pervades the present discussion too, as I even attempt to talk about the history of the process in which feminists of the dominant culture have been engaged. How to name the reality without colluding in it in this manner eludes me!) The second aspect of the violence is that such cooptation in fact continues the colonial project, even while claiming to try to put a stop to it. Spivak identifies the problem in this way:

> When we speak for ourselves, we urge with conviction; the personal is also political. For the rest of the world's women, the sense of whose personal micrology is difficult (though not impossible) for us to acquire, we fall back on a colonialist theory of most efficient information retrieval (Spivak 1988b: 179).

The problem of autonomy or agency of voice becomes even more complex. The very notion that we are in a position to 'let' other women speak for themselves maintains them in their role as 'subalterns'. Their speech is still instrumental to others' projects, even as that speech itself is channelled through the research and analyses of those others. On the contrary, however, when a 'subaltern' speaks, the very act of their speech itself terminates that relational description (their identity as 'subalterns') and spells the end of the colonial project it expresses (Spivak 1988a: 66-111).

Grasping some of these subtler expressions of our collusion in the role of oppressor as well as oppressed has been difficult for

feminists of the dominant culture. Recognizing the latter role
threatens more than does the former our claim to scholarly commitment to 'truth' in the sense of demonstrable accuracy in our
work, since the perspectival colonialism in which we are invested
results in a distorted picture. That distortion threatens our moral
identity as well as our academic sense of self, in that it betrays our
feminist commitment to do 'advocacy' scholarship, as an expression of what Jorge Pixley calls 'militant biblical scholarship'
(Pixley 1996: 74).

   The rubric of 'colonialism' is helpful in unmasking the decep-
tion in which we participate as victims and victimizers, because
that rubric expresses the systemic nature of the overall project.
That recognition overcomes the simple dichotomies of oppressor
and oppressed, evil and wronged, 'bad' and 'good'. The guilt we
carry for our reinforcement of that system is not the guilt of overt
malice (which we can quickly deny behind the defense of our
'liberal' or even 'radical' credentials), but rather the evil of collusion in a project that encompasses us and that, insofar as it
benefits us, we find untroubling. As with any system, however, to
jar it at one point moves the whole. Thus, as we begin to recognize that what has us enthralled is a colonial project, we can
perhaps begin to recognize how the project as a whole—where we
are at once colonized and colonizers—influences our lives in
general and our work as interpreters of the Bible in particular.
Perhaps even we can take some initial steps to change the work-
ings of that system.

The 'Post(-)Colonial' Project

'Postcolonial' is a term that suggests an optimistic standpoint relative to the project of political, military, economic, pedagogical
and ideological domination of one culture or people by another.
Just as the colonial project itself has material and discursive
dimensions, so the postcolonial response names both concrete
changes in the resources that shape daily life and the processes by
which they are allocated, on the one hand, and in the narratives
and other codes by which meaning is ascribed, on the other
(Mishra and Hodge 1991: 276-90; Donaldson 1992: 88-89; Spivak
1990: 1). The term 'postcolonial' suggests that the old colonial

project has ended, and the new designs that give shape to independence and self-determination are being crafted. Within postcolonial theory itself, however, there is a debate whether the term signifies only places, peoples and periods from which the colonizers have been expelled, or whether the term means 'after the on-set of colonialism' (Lionnet 1995: 4).

Both possible meanings are problematical when considering women's colonized status, however, for our captivity under the project of kyriarchy apparently began so long ago that it is scarcely possible to recover glimpses of times or places or peoples that could in the fullest sense be precolonial. Thus, identifying a time of the 'onset' of that particular expression of colonialism is difficult. Furthermore, to claim now to be living in a period or place where its dominance has been broken—despite the obviously greater options available to women of Western societies today than were available to our ancestors—would be naive. To think in temporal categories appears unproductive.

Colonial reality, however, in whatever form it takes, is always a reality of domination and of resistance. In the colonization of Abya Yala—a Kuna word meaning 'Mature Land', which refers collectively to the lands of the Western Hemisphere—the moment a conquistador's foot hit the shore and the imposition of cultural, religious and economic domination began, so too did strategies small and great for survival on those same fronts. Women's subversion and defiance of the kyriarchal project has been similar. That project has been effective in establishing economic, political, educational and religious institutions and practices that worked for the benefit of elite males, and in describing and analyzing the world in a way that inscribed the logic of their domination into the very narratives and laws (scientific as well as legal) that authenticated that domination. Nevertheless, in the midst of that domination women have been writing the world in a different way and have been discerning means for economic, political, cultural and spiritual survival in defiance of the attempt to write and enact them out of existence, or at least to confine them to the margins of its pages.

The Bible has played an ambiguous role in the subversive project of women relative to the kyriarchal colonial project. On the one hand, the Bible has provided powerful encoding of women's colonized status. Women's stories in any form are scarce in the Bible, and where women are mentioned, it is only as they relate to the purposes of the male authors and editors and of the religious authorities who made decisions about canonization. Traditional appropriations of the Bible, whether through ecclesial or academic channels, have further alienated the Bible from women's lives by the methodologies, hermeneutics and ideologies by which the appropriation has been carried forward. In spite of all that, however, the Bible has also provided women with comfort and strength often denied to them elsewhere in their lives. It has thus been as much a part of women's resistant lives of post-colonial protest as it has been an instrument of colonial domination (Lionnet 1995: 9-11; O'Brien Wicker 1993: 370; Comaroff 1985: 1-2). Women reading the Bible have tested to the limits Audre Lourde's contention that 'the master's tools will never dismantle the master's house' (Lourde 1981: 99), and the jury has not yet returned a final verdict in the case.

Guest Lists and Seating Charts: A Reading of Luke 14.1, 7-14

Introduction

The following study attempts to pursue questions implied in that unresolved verdict through an exploration of feminist and post-colonial critical perspectives relative to the teachings on banquet etiquette in Luke 14. The study examines the values, assumptions and social standpoints encoded in the narrative itself and the intersection of the text with various categories of women's lives, both in the ancient world and among modern readers. The movement through the study can be seen as a sort of fugue in which these two loci or 'themes' intertwine and take their turn as the dominant melody. The first of these themes entails the reading of the text itself. The second requires that we look at the reader reading the text, to discern what questions are and are not asked, what details are and are not taken into account, and what experiences or perspectives give rise both to the asking and the ignorance, the seeing and the not-seeing. To highlight the fugal pattern of the discussion, I have used different typefaces for the two 'themes'—roman type when the passage and its social world are in the foreground, and italic type when attention shifts to the reader—in this case one committed to a reading that is postcolonial and feminist, carried out from the perspective of a woman from the dominant culture of the United States.

Engaging the Text and the Reader

Luke places this episode near the mid-point of his narrative of Jesus' journey to Jerusalem. Just prior to this episode, the narrator's summary statement in 13.22, Jesus' retort to the threat from Herod (13.31-33), and his lament over the city's past and future (13.34-35), provide the first reminders of the goal of Jesus' journey since its beginning (9.51, 53). The episode itself is set at a religious festival (a Sabbath meal) in the home of a leader of the Pharisees, a group recognizable in the larger narrative as often opposed to the project Jesus announces, and occasionally to Jesus himself (for example, 5.21, 30; 6.1-5, 6-11; 11.53-54; 15.2; see Tannehill 1986: 183). The holy time and potentially hostile setting form a paradox to be echoed in the action, for in 14.1 the narrator implies that the host has invited Jesus to dine but reports close surveillance of him, as if the invitation itself were a set-up. In the style of a great teacher, Jesus turns the trap around, to snare instead the hunter who becomes the prey.

The setting evokes the picture of a dinner party whose host and guests are adept and successful players in the contest to establish honor and avoid shame, which appears to have marked the lives of well-to-do members of Luke's society. The order and logic of that usual contest, however, are subverted at a number of points. The gathering is first confronted with the sudden appearance of a man suffering from edema (14.2-6), a literary parallel to the earlier story of the bent-over women whom Jesus is said also to have healed on the Sabbath (13.10-17). The presence of this man occasions an exchange between Jesus and 'the lawyers and Pharisees' about the appropriateness of healing him on the Sabbath. Jesus' reading of the Law resolves the case in his favor, but within the framework of the lawyers' definition of how such actions could be justified.

Two details of this initial scene anchor the episode firmly in the assumptions of elite groups in Luke's world. The first relates to the life of the religious elite. The host follows what was apparently part of the Pharisees' charitable practice of opening their homes

to poor people of the community, who then could avail themselves of food left from the meal. By this practice the poor people
would be fed, and at the same time the host, who in obedience to
Torah would already have given the required tithe of the
resources represented in the meal, would be demonstrating his
righteousness through the additional charity. The second detail
identifies this meal with the experience of the social and economic upper class. Though apparently the meal has not yet been
served (for in 14.7 the guests are described by the imperfect tense
of the verb as in process of selecting their seats), the debate about
the Law (14.3, 5-6) follows the form of after-dinner symposia in
which both Jewish and Gentile participants in banquets—festive
meals that presupposed a degree of leisure for all participants as
well as of economic resources for the host—commonly engaged
during the Greco-Roman era.

   The only characters specifically identified in the story thus far
are Jesus, the host and the man who is healed. All are males. The
lawyers too are probably men. It is not clear whether women are
to be understood as present also, either among the guests or as
co-hosts. Whether they might have been depends to some extent
on whether this meal should be considered as private or public. A
Sabbath meal in someone's home seems, on the one hand, to be a
private meal, in which case women might well have been assumed
to be present. The number of guests (Jesus and his followers as
well as the lawyers) and the symposia-like discussions, both about
the appropriateness of the healing (14.3-6) and in the subsequent
teachings and parable (14.7-13, 14-24), however, move it more
into the genre of a public meal. Women generally did not attend
such meals, particularly when they would not have been included
as entertainers or sexual servants of the invited guests—a role
inconsistent with the identification of this as a Sabbath meal in a
Jewish home (Corley 1993: 66-75). The resulting picture is
ambiguous, and in the end it is not clear whether we should envision the women as present at all, if only during the actual sharing
of the food (Corley 1993: 24-79), or whether the masculine end-
ings and pronouns that characterize the story should be seen as
indicating a banquet for men only, where women might be found
only in the kitchen or serving at the table. Rightly or wrongly,
without explicit mention of women's *presence*, women's *absence* is

usually assumed (as indeed Kathleen Corley appears to do by not mentioning this episode in her study of women and meals in Luke [Corley 1993: 108-46]). Even if women are assumed to be present in this story, however, it is clear that they are narratively invisible and thus unimportant to the agenda being developed by the author at this point in the Gospel.

From the very beginning of the story, the house where the dinner is held is described as belonging to the male host. The fact that it is nowhere called 'their' home raises a question about the family structure assumed in the story, and about laws governing the ownership of real-estate. Is there a wife, and would the house not be considered hers also, either legally or socially? Are there children in the household? Servants? Logic suggests that the household would have included such persons. Why, then, does the author not deem their roles worth mentioning among the dramatis personae? Where should we envision these various groups of characters on the narrative stage? *Readers who find ourselves mirrored most closely in these groups of characters by virtue of our gender or social roles find our imaginations engaged by questions about such unmentioned characters, as well as or instead of by those more central to the agenda of the text.*

Women from the dominant culture in the West notice a fundamental disjunction between the assumptions underlying the passage and those of our own lives concerning women's place relative to banquets and table etiquette. To begin with, our customs of both public and private meals take for granted the presence of women and men alike among the guests. As a result, we often overlook women's invisibility in the text and do not question women's presence. In contrast, many women from Asia, Africa, and Latin America whose experience includes the exclusion of at least some women from the initial serving of festive meals or banquets recognize immediately that kyriarchal assumptions about women's roles and place require that one raise the question of women's participation relative to this episode.

Furthermore, in contrast to the assumptions encoded in the narrative and the ancient social world to which it bears witness, women in the West read this part of the Gospel narrative as particularly related to matters of concern to us. In our society it is women who worry about seating arrangements and guest lists at social occasions. Thus, the natural reading in the dominant culture of the West is a reading against *the gender*

*assumptions of the text. The ease with which Western women read this as
our story, however, makes the exclusive assumptions underlying the narrative even harder to identify. They simply do not register in our consciousness.*

Following the healing, the guests are portrayed as vying for
places at the banquet that will reflect best on themselves. Their
eagerness to win in the competition for the greatest honor sets
them up as the next group ripe for confrontation by Jesus. The
first counsel is prudence: do not leave yourself open to the shame
of being invited to move down to a place of lower status (Fitzmyer
1985: 1043). The narrator assumes that his implied audience will
concur in that prudence, and indeed we too nod in agreement. It
makes sense! No-one would choose to embarrass him- or herself if
that could be avoided.

What *is* avoided in the counsels of prudence in 14.7-11, however, is a shift of point of view away from that of the invited guests
to that of others in the household where the banquet is being
held. The truly 'lowest place' (14.10) is not at the table at all, but
in the kitchen and among those who serve the meal—probably
slaves or other servants in this leader's household, among the
poorer sectors of the society, and probably women of the family
(Seim 1994: 61). By omitting to raise this issue, Luke has already
revealed his assumptions about the perspective of his implied
audience: they too are people whose usual place is at the table,
and their concerns about relative honor relate to placement
there. The cooks and the waiters, and those who identify with
their roles in a banquet, look in from the margins of the narrative, as they do at the meal itself.

With 14.12 the status of the guests within the narrative becomes
even clearer. They are of a status where they too could host a
dinner party, for they are implied to be peers—friends, brothers,
relatives or rich neighbors—of the host who is directly addressed.
As hosts they are no longer urged to follow what common sense
recognizes as prudent. Rather, they are to jettison considerations
of reciprocity and honor given and received, and to change their
guest lists to include persons explicitly excluded from holy functions (the Aaronic priesthood [Lev. 21.17-23], the army of the
holy war [1QM 7.4-6] and membership in the Qumran community [1QSa 2.5-22]; see Ringe 1985: 58-59; Fitzmyer 1985: 1047), as

well as from 'society' dinners. Those to be invited are those identified as the ones to whom the good news of Jesus' words and actions is particularly addressed (4.18; 7.22), and who are to be the honored guests at the banquet of God's reign (14.15, 21).

Persons from dominant groups in any culture, and members of the dominant culture of the West generally accept quite easily the assumptions of the guests and hosts in the narrative—that people are seated in 'proper' places according to whatever categories are dictated by the specific occasion (such as one's relationship to the bride and groom at a wedding, or one's position in the corporate hierarchy in a banquet related to one's work), and that social events create and repay social obligations. Our circumstances, that make such assumptions self-evident, lead us, in a sense, to read the text 'correctly'—experiencing its affront to our normal practices of etiquette and hospitality. While we would probably readily dismiss the validity of religious exclusion or the rejection of women's presence from such a setting, we might well accept a host's right not to invite those they do not choose to, or those who might make other guests uncomfortable. So much at home are women from such groups in adjudicating such matters, and so clearly do we recognize ourselves as those whose role it is to make such decisions in our own homes and families' lives, that we fail to notice that we ourselves are probably among the people relegated to the kitchen or otherwise on the margins of this story. On these grounds too, we simply read ourselves in, and assume that we belong.

Although the criteria of honor implied to be self-evident to the characters in the narrative are rejected by the Gospel writer's perspective, the goal of acquiring honor is not questioned. The honor to which these characters are now to aspire is that conveyed by their reward 'at the resurrection of the righteous'. In addition to accepting the legitimacy of the quest for honor (as its locus is redefined), the narrative also leaves unquestioned the right of access to that honor, which belongs to these members of the social elite if only they use their resources appropriately. They still remain those whose concern is at the table, and who adjudicate access to it. The fact that the narrative does not raise such questions confirms the suggestion already glimpsed in the teachings of 14.7-11, that Luke's implied audience—and possibly Luke himself—shared the identity of the characters in the story. The assumptions of the world of the social elites of societies under the hegemony of Rome, and the elites' assumptions that they hold

their rightful place in it, remain intact. It is still they who determine guest lists and seating charts—access to the 'banquet'—and
who, by following the new rules, can assure their continued places
of honor. Thus, in the final analysis, although the specific behav-
ioral requirements have shifted radically in the direction of
greater inclusiveness in conformity to other teachings about those
to whom the good news of God's reign is directed, these teachings
fit with the diners', Luke's audience's and our own self-image as
able to fulfill the demands of God's righteousness as 'Lords and
Ladies Bountiful'. Charity and not fundamental systemic change
is the key to the divine project envisioned by this section of Luke's
Gospel, and with charity comes collusion in basic aspects of the
world-view that sustained the Roman Empire *and sustains the
various imperial or colonial projects of our own day.* While the passage
functions as a challenge to existing social codes and values, it
appeals to its audience *and to us in terms we understand because of our
place in the very system under challenge.*

*The story as it is presented in Luke plays into our own desire to link acts
of charity to an assessment of our religious worth, though admittedly such
stories as this bring persons who are seen as objects of charity uncomfort-
ably close to home! What is assumed is a religion based* de facto *on works
of righteousness, performed as part of a game we play with skill acquired
through long practice as persons of economic and social privilege. What is
called for by the text is the posture of the gracious and generous host, and
that standard we could surely meet. Persons not in an economic or social
position to play such a role, on the other hand, readily recognize the exclu-
siveness of the assumptions that undergird this story. They read from
around the edges of the banquet room, recognizing full well that such
criteria of righteousness do not pertain to them. They perceive readily what
ambiguously located self-interest has taught us to ignore.*

Conclusion
*The fact of the matter is that this text itself participates in the discursive
expression of the colonial project of kyriarchy that characterizes the social
world of Luke and our own world as well. The text further provides legitimation for that project by giving it a religious benediction in words
attributed to Jesus. The foundational assumption of the text that we
instinctively accept is that we play the role of the host—the ones who decide
the date and place of the party, the menu, the size and shape of the table,*

and who is or is not invited. The text challenges those of us with power to mitigate the practices of colonial authority, but it does not dismantle that authority or fundamentally challenge the exclusive and hierarchical allocation of its power and benefits.

A postcolonial and feminist reading of the story requires that we begin to deconstruct the systemic logic that accords the right to issue or withhold invitations, or otherwise to control access to goods, services, power, and dignity on the basis of colonial criteria. Such a reading also poses the interim question of how we are to live in the meantime, in those situations where our gender, race, class, nationality, or other factor has placed us in positions of power, or where we have been invited as 'tokens' to tables set by others. Banquet tables ostensibly for fun and the celebration of our success and acceptance become for us work tables where we learn a method of resistant reading that breaks through the 'trained incapacity' that is the product of our ambivalent status as colonized and colonizers at the same time. This resistant reading allows us to move at a tangent to this text, reading with *its announced values, but* against *the contrary system it embodies— a movement that, like this study, has the pattern of a fugue, and characterizes our very lives.*

BIBLIOGRAPHY

Ashcroft, Bill, Gareth Griffiths and Helen Tiffin (eds.)
    1995   *The Post-Colonial Studies Reader* (New York: Routledge & Kegan Paul).
Brewster, Anne
    1995   *Literary Formations: Postcolonialism, Nationalism, Globalism* (Melbourne: University Press).
Burke, Kenneth
    1984   *Permanence and Change: An Anatomy of Purpose* (Berkeley: University of California Press, 3rd edn).
Comaroff, Jean
    1985   *Body of Power, Spirit of Resistance: The Culture and History of a South African People* (Chicago: University of Chicago Press).
Corley, Kathleen C.
    1993   *Private Women, Public Meals: Social Conflict in the Synoptic Tradition* (Peabody, MA: Hendrickson).
Donaldson, Laura E.
    1992   *Decolonizing Feminisms: Race, Gender, and Empire-Building* (Chapel Hill: University of North Carolina Press).
Fitzmyer, Joseph A.
    1985   *The Gospel According to Luke X–XXIV* (AB, 28A; Garden City, NY: Doubleday).

Guha, Ranajit, and Gayatri Chakravorty Spivak (eds.)
    1988   *Selected Subaltern Studies* (New York: Oxford University Press).
Hutcheon, Linda
    1995 [1989] 'Circling the Downspout of Empire', in Bill Ashcroft, Gareth
            Griffiths and Helen Tiffin (eds.), *The Post-Colonial Studies Reader*
            (New York: Routledge & Kegan Paul): 130-35.
Landry, Donna, and Gerald MacLean (eds.)
    1996   *The Spivak Reader: Selected Works of Gayatri Chakravorty Spivak* (New
            York: Routledge & Kegan Paul).
Lashgari, Deirdre (ed.)
    1995   *Violence, Silence, and Anger: Women's Writing as Transgression* (Char-
            lottesville: University Press of Virginia).
Lionnet, Françoise
    1995   *Postcolonial Representations: Women, Literature, Identity* (Ithaca, NY:
            Cornell University Press).
Lourde, Audrey
    1981   'The Master's Tools Will Never Dismantle the Master's House', in C.
            Morraga and G. Anzalda (eds.), *The Bridge Called my Back: Writings by
            Radical Woman of Colour* (Waterdown, MA: Persephone Press): 99.
Mishra, Vijay, and Bob Hodge
    1994 [1991] 'What is Post(-)Colonialism?', in Patrick Williams and Laura Chris-
            man (eds.), *Colonial Discourse and Post-Colonial Theory: A Reader* (New
            York: Columbia University Press, 1994): 276-90.
Mohanty, Chandra Talpade
    1995 [1984] 'Under Western Eyes: Feminist Scholarship and Colonial Discours-
            es', in Bill Ashcroft, Gareth Griffiths and Helen Tiffin (eds.), *The
            Post-Colonial Studies Reader* (New York: Routledge & Kegan Paul):
            259-63.
O'Brien Wicker, Kathleen
    1993   'Teaching Feminist Biblical Studies in a Postcolonial Context', in
            Elisabeth Schüssler Fiorenza (ed.), *Searching the Scriptures: A Feminist
            Introduction*, I (New York: Crossroad): 367-80.
Pixley, Jorge
    1996   'Toward a Militant Biblical Scholarship', *Bib Int* 4.1: 72-75.
Prakash, Gyan (ed.)
    1995   *After Colonialism: Imperial Histories and Postcolonial Displacements*
            (Princeton, NJ: Princeton University Press).
Ringe, Sharon H.
    1985   *Jesus, Liberation, and the Biblical Jubilee: Images for Ethics and Christology*
            (Philadelphia: Fortress Press).
Sakenfeld, Katharine Doob
    1988   'Feminist Perspectives on Bible and Theology: An Introduction to
            Selected Issues and Literature', *Int* 42.1: 5-18.
Schüssler Fiorenza, Elisabeth
    1994   *Jesus: Miriam's Child, Sophia's Prophet: Critical Issues in Feminist Chris-
            tology* (New York: Crossroad).

Seim, Turid Karlsen
    1994   *The Double Message: Patterns of Gender in Luke and Acts* (Nashville: Abingdon Press).

Spivak, Gayatri Chakravorty
    1994 [1988a] 'Can the Subaltern Speak?', in Patrick Williams and Laura Chrisman (eds.), *Colonial Discourse and Post-Colonial Theory: A Reader* (New York: Columbia University Press): 66-111.
    1988b   *In Other Worlds: Essays in Cultural Politics* (New York: Routledge & Kegan Paul).
    1988c   'Subaltern Studies: Deconstructing Historiography', in Ranajit Guha and Gayatri Chakravorty Spivak (eds.), *Selected Subaltern Studies* (New York: Oxford University Press): 3-32.
    1990   *The Post-Colonial Critic: Interviews, Strategies, Dialogues* (ed. Sarah Harasym; New York: Routledge & Kegan Paul).
    1993   *Outside in the Teaching Machine* (New York: Routledge & Kegan Paul).

Tannehill, Robert C.
    1986   *The Narrative Unity of Luke–Acts: A Literary Interpretation*. I. *The Gospel According to Luke* (Philadelphia: Fortress Press).

Trinh, T. Minh-ha
    1989   *Woman, Native, Other: Writing Postcoloniality and Feminism* (Bloomington: Indiana University Press).

Williams, Patrick, and Laura Chrisman (eds.)
    1994   *Colonial Discourse and Post-Colonial Theory: A Reader* (New York: Columbia University Press).

Submerged Biblical Histories and Imperial Biblical Studies

RICHARD A. HORSLEY

'One of the distinct effects of the recent emergence of postcolonial criticism has been to force a radical re-thinking and re-formulation of forms of knowledge and social identities authored and authorized by colonialism and western domination' (Prakash 1992: 8). It has therefore 'created a ferment in the field of knowledge'. One may hope that such a ferment will spread more fully into biblical studies, which remain as solidly under the hegemony of Euro-American traditions as any other academic field. It may be more difficult than in other fields for post-colonial criticism to counter the dominant Eurocentrism and the emergent North American hegemony in established biblical studies. A major obstacle may be the prominent role that the Bible played in modern colonial relations. The Bible came to African, Asian, and (indigenous) American peoples almost always as part of the colonizers' religion, as the sacred Scripture that provided divine sanction and legitimation for imperial domination and oppression (e.g. Kwok 1989). Ironically, of course, modern African and Asian peoples (like medieval European peasants before them and Afro-American slaves and Latin American campesinos beside them) discerned that biblical literature speaks with various voices (e.g. Mosala 1989; Weems 1991). Underneath the cooptive overwriting of the literate elite responsible for the authoritative final 'Scripture' are narratives of liberation and songs of resistance. Ironically, the very missionary schools which taught the Bible, translated into the 'natives'' languages, produced many an anti-colonial agitator. It has taken nearly another two generations, however, for the entrenched field of biblical studies to realize what has happened and to be ready to listen to emergent scholarly voices from formerly colonized peoples to reflect upon the role of biblical literature and history in colonial and postcolonial relations.

A major result of precisely such reflection has been increasing recognition of the degree to which those liberative narratives, songs, and proclamations have been overlaid by domesticating disciples (deutero-Paulines), evangelists ('Luke'), scribal schools (Deuteronomistic historians) and creeds (formulated by imperially directed church councils). In a fascinating turn of events, postcolonial criticism of prevailing politico-economic and cultural relations in the modern world makes it possible to discern, often for the very first time, the concrete ways in which the various layers in biblical literature are the products of the very emergence of (struggle for) domination and authority. As ancient authority figures assumed the authority to overwrite various traditions into a version that authorized their own authority, so modern colonized readers are assuming the authority to unearth previously submerged biblical voices and histories that undermine the self-authorization of ancient authorities as well as their authoritarian modern colonial beneficiaries. But once we discern those previously submerged voices, stories, songs, etc., what do we make of them? In what context do we hear or read them?

Critics of postcolonial discourse charge it with being 'complicitous in the consecration of hegemony' (Shohat 1992: 110; Dirlik 1994: 331; Ahmad 1992). 'Postcolonial' as a description of the world situation in the late twentieth century 'mystifies both politically and methodologically' a current reconfiguration of earlier forms of domination in the neoimperialism of global capital. 'Postcolonialism' may often divert attention from contemporary problems of social, political, and cultural domination and obfuscate its own relationship to the conditions of its own emergence, that is to a global capitalism that structures global economic, political, and cultural relations.

We obviously do not want our postcolonial criticism that aims to resist and undo colonial cultural hegemony to become, in effect, complicitous in consecrating the new global capitalist domination by our failure to address the latter's mechanisms and our relations to it. Similarly, we do not want our postcolonial criticism that aims to emancipate previously submerged biblical stories and histories to fail to take into account the imperial situation in and over against which those stories and histories emerged. Indeed, perhaps by discerning the ancient imperial context of biblical materials in order better to appreciate their agenda we can be more critically prepared to 'read' the current postcolonial or neo-imperial situation in which we want to intervene.

Biblical studies as a field, of course, is one of many products of modern Western imperial culture and its 'orientalism', but with a few interesting twists. Like modern Western imperialist or nationalist historiography generally, biblical studies effectively obscured or submerged the histories and aspirations of imperially subjected peoples. This effect can be discerned in several interrelated aspects of biblical studies as an established modern academic field. Most striking perhaps was its reduction of literature that clearly deals with all aspects of life (political, economic, religious, historical—all as inseparable) to merely its religious aspect. Western biblical scholars studied the Bible primarily for the theology it would yield. This enterprise corresponded to the Western (particularly Protestant) reduction of religion to personal faith. Not surprisingly, therefore, just as Western imperial culture and political practice constructed an 'Orient' as its Other (Said 1978), theologically determined biblical studies fabricated a parochial-political and legalistic-ritualistic 'Judaism' as an Other-religion over against true, universal and purely spiritual religion: Western European Christianity. In this connection, biblical studies constructed religious history according to a set of essentialist dichotomies that parallel those of Western colonialism/orientalism: Christian versus Jewish, Hellenistic versus Jewish, wisdom versus apocalyptic, and so on.

As part of Western culture which constructed a dividing wall between the humanizing realm of culture and the practical world of politics, moreover, New Testament studies in particular systematically depoliticized particular biblical books and the authors or movements that produced them. In the theologically determined metanarrative of the field, the replacement of the overly political and particularistic religion 'Judaism' by the purely spiritual and universal religion 'Christianity', furthermore, rendered virtually irrelevant the overall imperial situation and particular colonial relations in response to which those movements and writings emerged.

Perhaps most determinative of all for modern New Testament studies' submersion of subject people's history and aspirations, was its reading of the Gospels and Paul's letters as the founding documents of Western Christianity, as the beginnings of the history of Western Christian civilization. This is the height of irony, since historically the Gospels, Paul's letters and the book of Revelation were the literature of peoples subjected to a Western empire. This literature proclaimed, in the Christ events, God's inauguration of a new age that would imminently replace the Roman imperial order and that God's fulfilment of history had run through a subjected 'Third World' people, Israel, rather than through the history of Greece and Rome.

The agenda of postcolonial discourse appears to be, variously, to give voice in the central sites of Euro-American cultural criticism to subjects from previously colonized areas. More broadly and particularly, postcolonial discourse aims to emancipate previously submerged (colonized) histories and identities and, in the process, to reveal the complex hybridity and contingency of peoples in the contemporary world. A postcolonial (and anti-imperial) biblical studies includes in its agenda the emancipation of previously submerged or distorted histories of the movements that produced the literature that was later included in the Bible—partly by avoiding, opposing, and replacing the essentialist and depoliticizing categories and approaches of imperial Western biblical studies.

Once we recognize that New Testament literature is in fact not written to and for those situated in the metropolises of a Western empire it becomes apparent that in many significant respects a Mark and a Paul in their own way parallel and prepare the way for today's postcolonial writers and scholars. I would like to explore some of the ways in which Mark and Paul not only resist the dominant imperial culture in their writing, but proceed with the restoration or building of communities alternative to the imperial order in the movements for which they are spokespersons.

Mark

From the postcolonial perspective the means by which Western
biblical studies claimed the Gospel of Mark in support of the
grand narrative of Western Christianity become readily evident.
European theologians relied upon Western Christian traditions
that 'Mark' was an associate of Peter, founder of the church in the
imperial metropolis of Rome. The Gospel was located in Rome,
addressed to the church in the imperial metropolis, thus legiti-
mating its modern reading from the corresponding imperial
metropolitan sites. The dominant scholarly reading of Mark as a
passion narrative with a long introduction dissolved all of the
Galilean 'local color' and the Galilean prophet's confrontation
with the Judean rulers in Jerusalem into incidental stage-setting
for the Hellenistic Christian crucifixion-resurrection kerygma that
became the basis of established Western Christianity.

More recently several twentieth-century, Western theological
readings of Mark have served to obscure the anti-imperial political
plot of the Gospel. Once Western scholars focused on the pre-
Jerusalem narrative in Mark as no more than a long 'introduction' to the passion narrative, they similarly dissolved it into
Western essentialist theology. The voyages back and forth across
the Sea of Galilee symbolized Jesus' joining of the 'Gentile' and
'Jewish' sides in the 'Christian' universalism that replaced 'Jewish'
particularism (Kelber 1974). Never mind that the Gospel itself
gives no indication of 'Jewish' and 'Gentile' sides of the Sea, let
alone any reference to 'Judaism'. Individualistic Western Christians persist in reading Mark as a 'discipleship' narrative in which
the disciples, particularly Peter, exhibit all of the misunder-
standings and lapses as well as commitment and devotion typical
of a distinctively Western type of Christian discipleship. Meanwhile Jesus' prophetic agenda throughout the Gospel and particularly his confrontation with the Roman client rulers and their
condemnation and execution of him as a rebel leader retreat into
the background again as incidental stage setting for the central
drama of the typical 'disciple's' struggle between doubt/denial/
guilt and repentance/forgiveness/recommitment.

A postcolonial reading of Mark's narrative, however, makes it
appear much like the sort of history that recent subaltern studies

are striving to construct of the Indian peasantry. Not only does
nothing in Mark suggest an orientation to the imperial metropolis
or to universalism or to devotional individualism, Mark's narrative
in fact indicates the virtual opposites of these modern Western
impositions on the text. Written from an out-of-the-way site of a
people only recently subjected by the Empire and not particularly
civilized, Mark sharply opposes both alien imperial rule and its
collaborators among the local 'colonial' aristocracy. Remote from
the universalizing discourse of Western imperial culture, Mark
strives to build on the subject people's history and revitalize its
traditions. Indeed, Mark exhorts an indigenous people's movement of resistance to the imperial order to embody an alternative
social order, understood as the fulfilment of history of that (now)
subjected people of Israel.

The narrative's own orientation forces recognition of its
'colonial' location and anti-imperial agenda. Far from addressing
individuals in a metropolis, Mark speaks from and for a subject
people in opposition to institutions in an imperial order. In contrast with Luke–Acts, in which the Jesus movement moves systematically and relentlessly from Jerusalem, the site of (Roman client)
Judean rule, to Rome, the seat of Empire itself, Mark calls
hearers/readers in the movement back to the villages of Galilee
(presumably to continue the project inaugurated in Jesus' ministry; 14.23; 16.7). Jesus and his movement take an active and
uncompromising stance against the temple-state in Jerusalem.
From the beginning of his ministry his activities and articulations
are threatening to the authorities (1.21-28), who plot 'how to
destroy him' (3.6, 22; 12.12-14). The Empire appears in Mark
directly only in the form of Caesar demanding tribute and his
governor and soldiers, who execute Jesus as an insurrectionary
(12.14; 15.1-32). Mark's Gospel, written from the site and perspective of a subject people at some distance from the metropolis,
stands against both the Empire and its client Judean and Galilean
rulers, Antipas and the high priests.

Far from being universalistic, Mark draws upon and gives new
life to the traditions of a particular people, Israel. Mark thus revi-
talizes the history of a people whose origins lay in escape from
and revolt against ancient Near Eastern kings and empires, a people moreover who, although subjected to a series of empires for

many centuries, still pursued its traditional way of life in Galilean, Samaritan, and Judean villages. More particularly, Mark stands not in what anthropologists have called the 'great tradition' of the Judean scribes and their temple-state sponsors, but in the 'little' or popular tradition of the Galilean peasantry. Mark's Jesus and his followers are informed by distinctively Israelite traditions of leadership, those of the great prophetic founders and renewers of the people, Moses and Elijah. Jesus performs the actions of the new Moses–Elijah, with sea-crossings, exorcisms, healings and wilderness feedings (see esp. Mk 4.35–8.26; 9.2-8). Although it is less integral to the stories he incorporates into his overall narrative, Mark also adapts the distinctively Israelite 'script' of a popular Messiah, acclaimed by the people as the leader of their independence from human rulers, but then captured and executed by the imperial rulers (see esp. Mk 8.27-30; 11.2-20). Struggle in Mark's Gospel is the particular one of Israel over against what is ostensibly its own priestly aristocratic and royal leadership, who had long since become creatures of the Empire. It is a people's struggle, not a general story of individual salvation or illumination. Those exorcised or healed—for example, the woman who had been hemorrhaging for 12 years and the 12-year-old woman who was near death just as she approached the age for reproductive life—are not simply particular persons, but are representative of the whole people and its malaise (see esp. Mk 5.21-43).

Mark not only renews Israelite traditions, but nurtures and grounds a concrete movement engaged in revitalizing Israelite society in its fundamental social forms of family and village covenantal community (10.2-31, 41-44).[1] The only character in the Gospel who approaches Jesus with an individualistic agenda appears as a foil for covenantal economic reciprocity—and departs out of his own rejection of the covenantal agenda that had been basic in Israel since Moses (10.17-22). Mark's Jesus implements a program of the renewal of Israel in appointing the Twelve as symbolic leaders of the people and in performing the series of Moses-and-Elijah-like actions that release the people from possession by the alien force of 'Legion', bring an end to the

1.   Students from Burma, the Philippines and South Africa who were far more closely in contact with peasant life than I was, pointed this out in a course at Harvard Divinity School in 1990.

woman's/Israel's hemorrhaging, and give new (re-)productive life
to the 12-year-old woman/Israel (5.1-20, 21-43). Not only does
Mark's Jesus insist upon the basic 'commandment of God'
('honor your father and mother') as the fundamental principle
guiding use of the people's land and productivity, over against the
temple-state's 'traditions of the elders' (7.9-13), he also (more)
programmatically, renews the egalitarian Mosaic covenantal
(social–economic–political) order of the Israelite peasantry,
giving explicit attention to marriage as the basis of family, egalitarian distribution of economic resources as the basis of family
and village life and egalitarian politics as the basis of communal
cooperation and solidarity (10.1-45). In the Last Supper, finally,
as the Messiah designate representative of Israel, he solemnly rit-
ualizes the renewed covenant between God and Israel ('this is my
blood of the covenant, poured out for many'; 14.22-25). Finally,
his execution in the Roman form used for slaves and insurrec-
tionaries becomes the martyrdom that seals the solidarity of the
movement (15.16-39). At the Last Supper and then in the open
ending of the Good News at the empty tomb, the hearers/readers
are directed back to Galilee to continue the project of renewal of
the people begun by Jesus (14.28; 16.7).

Thus, if the concrete particulars are not dissolved into abstract
theological generalizations, Mark's Good News is the (hi)story of
a concrete renewal movement of a people in resistance to imperial domination. While it is unmistakably a renewal of Israel, however, it is more than that, or more precisely something more than
Western New Testament studies have allowed as possible coming
from 'Judaism'. In their own version of 'orientalism', New Testament studies have projected an essentialist 'nationalism' onto
ancient Palestinian 'Judaism'. 'Nationalism' in its modern meaning, European or anti-colonial, is an utter anachronism with
regard to ancient Israelites. It is highly doubtful historically that
people living in ancient Galilee or Judea had come to identify
themselves in 'imagined communities' (Anderson 1991) of
'nations' or 'nation-states'. Jason of Cyrene's *ioudaismos* (in 2
Maccabees) and Paul's fanatical pursuit of *ioudaismos*, almost the
only attested occurrences of the concept, involved something like
a 'Kulturkampf'. The 'Jewish War' of 66–70 CE, however, was basically a sequential or sustained 'peasant revolt'. After the initial

popular eruption in Jerusalem, the principal groups in revolt
came from the peasantry in various regions of Palestine (the
'Zealots' from North-West Judea, with whom a handful of
Galileans temporarily allied themselves, Simon bar Giora's force
from South-East Judea and the Idumeans). As Josephus admits,
the only high priests and leading Pharisees who did not simply
flee Jerusalem were attempting to stall for time while seeking an
accommodation with the Romans. Thus we must be careful not to
impose modern 'nationalism' onto Mark and other expressions of
renewal movements grounded in Israelite traditions.

Mark's Gospel, however, suggests a movement similar to recent
anti-imperial 'nationalist' movements insofar as it sought an
'ideological basis for a wider unity than any known before' (Said
1994: 209-10). In modern anti-colonial movements this was necessary even after the period of 'primary resistance' in efforts to
reconstitute a 'shattered community, to save or restore the sense
and fact of community against all the pressures of the colonial
system' (Davidson 1978: 155). Like Fanon and certain other
recent leading anti-imperial thinkers, 'Mark' does not indulge in
idyllic fantasies. Mark's renewal of Israel was not 'ethnic'. Unlike
priestly or scribal guardians of 'purity' and privilege within Israel,
Mark's and other peasant movements had no motivation to maintain group boundaries. We have no idea—peasants left no literary
sources—whether they were aware of their own hybrid identity or
of the differences in 'ethnic' lineage from village to village, valley
to valley. The 'identity' of the popular ('little') Israelite tradition
had repeatedly manifested itself as open to and cooperative with
other peasantries in common opposition to rulers (e.g. narratives
in Joshua, Judges, 1–2 Samuel; eighth to seventh century
prophetic oracles). Mark has Jesus spreading the movement
across the imperial boundaries of client rulers' territories, from
the Galilee of Antipas to the 'villages' or 'regions' of Caesarea
Philippi, Tyre, the cities of the Decapolis, and finally into the
jurisdiction of the Jerusalem high priests under/and the Roman
governor Pilate (5.1; 7.24; 8.22, 27; 10.1). Not only were those
peoples not all Judeans, they were not all Israelites. And Mark,
most pointedly, makes the 'Syro-Phoenician' woman the only
person who bests Jesus in debate (7.24-30). Mark's Gospel and
movement are particularistic, as a renewal of Israel in Mosaic

covenantal community. But the Good News and the movement are expansive, seeking a 'wider unity' among other subject peoples. If exclusive, it is only of the rich who will find it difficult to 'enter the kingdom of God' (10.17-27). It is not clear that essential identity was ever strong among the Galilean Israelites among whom the Jesus movement began (Horsley 1995: Chapters 2–3). It could be that the idea of pursuing a movement of renewal for all-Israel (but an open Israel) was directly or indirectly provoked by the experience of being subject to Jerusalem rulers who claimed, against the popular Israelite tradition, to be legitimate rulers over Israel and/or by the recent Roman conquest and reconquest that had been particularly destructive in Galilee. Mark hardly displays universalism. But Mark is equally lacking in essentialist identity. Explicitly 'the kingdom of God' and implicitly covenantal equality and solidarity provide the principles of unity and unity in diversity. The idea of a wider unity in an Israelite-based movement of covenantal solidarity and resistance to the imperial order that reached out to other peoples was clearly a powerful driving force in the first generation of the Jesus movement(s) behind Mark and similar literary expressions.

Mark also provides a metanarrative that enables a movement to maintain its own identity and solidarity over against the pretensions of the imperial metanarrative.[2] As is often observed about recent movements of anti-imperial resistance, far from being merely a reaction to imperialism, Mark's Gospel was an alternative way of conceiving history. History was not running only or primarily through Rome and her empire, but God, who acted previously to deliver, establish and renew a people, is active again now in Jesus delivering and renewing people.

'The power to narrate, or to block other narratives from forming and emerging, is very important to culture and imperialism, and constitutes one of the main connections between them' (Said 1994: xiii). Established Christianity coopted Mark, and established Western biblical studies have effectively kept Mark's narrative of a submerged people's history of renewal from re-emerging.

---

2. Many postcolonial writers are suspicious and highly critical of all metanarratives. For an expression of concern that precinding from metanarratives might leave only disjointed mininarratives that would, in effect, reinforce the currently hegemonic worldview, see Coronil 1992: 99-100.

Reading Mark from a postcolonial perspective may enable the recovery of Mark as a narrative of imperially subjected peasantries forming a movement of revitalized cooperative social formations based on their own indigenous traditions of independence of both exploitative local ruling institutions and Western imperial domination.

Paul

Western Christianity's cooptation of Paul is surely European Christianity's and established biblical studies' paradigmatic essentialization, individualization and depoliticization of the Bible. Paul's letters must be the prototypical case of a history that was submerged by the West despite the fact that it was already clearly written and widely available for reading. What an irony that, when not obscured by Western theologically determined historiography, Paul's mission and letters appear insistently particularistic, so obsessed with both local and worldwide community that they discourage individualism, and highly political especially in their anti-imperial agenda.

The Reformation, followed by establishment biblical studies, consolidated the essentialization of Paul, who became both the founder of the Christian faith and a 'convert' to it. Of course, besides those being mutually contradictory (can one 'convert' to a faith that has yet to be formulated?), there was no such term or concept, much less historical reality as 'Christian' or 'Christianity' at the time of Paul. As an irony within the irony, authoritative and authorized Christian NT interpreters present as 'Christian', as the basis of an essential and stable identity, what was—in Paul's own experience as a diaspora Jew who dramatically, from one project to another in his letters, focused on the peculiar issues that came up in particular diverse communities, and in the reception of those letters by those communities who apparently did not comprehend or agree with what Paul was writing—painfully hybrid, mixed, amalgamated, utterly unstable and so on. Paul himself was apparently born in exile, a Judean (Benjaminite) in diaspora speaking Greek. He then became a fanatical fighter for *ioudaismos*, then became self-exiled in a double sense: joined a popular movement (of people beneath his own educated social status) and moved out to the peoples/Gentiles fully aware that such a move would seriously alienate him from other movement leaders as well as fellow 'Judeans'.

Augustine crystalized, and again Luther and his followers consolidated, Paul as the paradigmatic individual hero of faith, *homo religiosus*, who, obsessed with his own striving for perfection, finally surrendered his will in faith in Christ, a breakthrough that yielded a personal release, and freedom of the soon-to-be-sovereign individual person in the West. Similarly, it was the Reformation followed by modern Western theology that consolidated earlier division between the city of God and the city of mankind, the two kingdoms, temporal and spiritual power, and thoroughly depoliticized Paul. Or perhaps it would be more accurate to say that Paul was repoliticized, only in a conservative or even reactionary direction. His statements in Romans 13 were made into the divine sanction of rulers of all sorts as well as into the very paradigm of unquestioning obedience to the state.

Read from a postcolonial perspective, on the other hand, Paul appears to resemble more recent anti-colonial leaders or postcolonial intellectuals in important respects. Paul's message and mission have significant similarities with three interrelated features of 'decolonizing cultural resistance' (Said 1994: 215-16).

First, decolonizing writers insist on the right to see the(ir) community's history whole, to restore the imprisoned nation to itself.' Judean apocalyptic literature such as the *Apocalypse of Daniel*, the *Testament of Moses*, certain sections of *1 Enoch*, and certain sections of the *Psalms of Solomon*, offer visions that comprehend the history of imperial domination and anticipate the restoration of the people's sovereignty. The motive of Jason of Cyrene's five-book history of the Maccabean Revolt and of its abridgment into the book of 2 Maccabees was to use the successful Judean resistance to the Seleucid imperial regime as an inspiration for resistance by Jewish communities in Cyrenaica. Such resistance even by Jewish communities in the diaspora sheds light on the activities of Paul before he experienced his dramatic 'revelation of Christ'. 2 Maccabees provides almost the only attestation of the term *ioudaismos* prior to Paul's usage in his portrayal of his life prior to becoming Christ's apostle, in Gal. 1.14. The concept was apparently formulated as a counterpart to *hellenismos*, which referred to a programmatic pressing of Hellenistic

politico-cultural forms on subject peoples. Thus *ioudaismos* was the
defensive attempt to maintain the traditional way of life in the
adverse condition of imperial rule.

That is how we can understand Paul's explanation of his previous 'persecuting the assembly of God' and trying to destroy it: 'I
[had] advanced in *ioudaismos* beyond many among my people of
the same age, for I was far more zealous for the traditions of my
ancestors' (Gal. 1.13-14). Having come originally from the diaspora Jewish community in Tarsus (in southern Asia Minor), he
must have come to Jerusalem at a relatively young age. There he
became involved apparently with scribal circles dedicated to resisting Hellenistic-Roman imperialism with their own program of
rigorous adherence to the traditional way of life. That would have
meant some attempt at discipline in the wider Judean society and
diaspora communities. Agitation by the followers of Jesus must
have threatened to bring the Roman forces down against the
people, thus jeopardizing the longer-range program of waiting
out the Empire—or waiting for the propitious moment for assertion of independence—while maintaining discipline in the ranks
of their own people. Almost certainly Paul's apocalypticism preceded his 'apocalypse of Christ' experience (Gal. 1.13-18). That
Jewish apocalypticism provided the perspective from which he
could view the Roman Empire as limited by the grand divine plan
or 'mystery' as well as the motivation for disciplining the people
in anticipation of their eventual restoration of independence
under God's direct rule.

Second, that apocalyptic perspective provided a reflective and
aggressive intellectual such as Paul with the possibility of viewing
not simply resisting assimilation into Roman imperial culture
while awaiting the end of Roman rule. Like more recent
'decolonizing cultural resistance', Paul's Jewish apocalypticism
was 'an alternative way of conceiving human history' (Said 1994:
216). The (biblical) history of the people of Israel, which began in
escape from and resistance to the rule of Pharaoh and Canaanite
kings (Exod. 1–15; Josh. 8–12; Judg. 5) celebrated God's repeated
deliverance of the people and featured God's irrevocable threefold promise to Abraham. Indeed, God's will in world history was
supposedly working through Israel. Through Abraham's offspring
Israel would become a great people on her own land, and other

peoples would receive blessings as well (Gen. 12.1-3). As we know from the apocalyptic books they wrote, Paul's Jewish visionary predecessors insisted, against all appearances, that God was faithful to those promises. Eventual restoration of the people was certain. Ultimately, world history was running through the history of Israel; Roman rule could be placed in perspective as the most recent but the last empire before the fulfilment of God's ancient promises.

This apocalyptic sense of an alternative history, of course, is what 'set Paul up' for the 'revelation of Christ' that transformed his life from a persecutor to an apostle of Christ. We simply do not know the extent to which Paul's *ioudaismos* meant political as well as cultural resistance to Roman imperialism. It is clear, however, that once he became convinced that in Christ's crucifixion and exaltation God had inaugurated the fulfilment of history, the delivery of the promises to Abraham, he understood his own role to be not simply the preaching of the 'good news' of that fulfilment, but also the organizing of communities of people in anticipation of the imminent advent of direct divine rule. In contrast to recent 'decolonizing cultural resistance', Paul's project was more comprehensive in scope. Only because of the depoliticization Paul has undergone at the hands of Western 'Christianity' and modern biblical studies are his *ekklēsiai* understood as 'churches' and his project as the foundation of a new 'religion'. He understood the project in which he was engaged as the founding or 'building' of an alternative society. Yet because of his conviction that the Roman Empire was now being superseded by the fulfilment of history that had been running through Israel all along, he could move boldly out into the imperial world on his mission. In that regard he resembles recent 'decolonizing cultural resistance' in 'breaking down the barriers between cultures'. His own Gospel of an alternative history disrupted and replaced the Roman imperial narrative but did that through direct interaction with and bold borrowing from the dominant culture. He entered into and mixed with the discourse of the dominant Western metropolitan culture in order to transform it—in ways similar to many a postcolonial intellectual. Insofar as he preaches and, in his letters such as 1 Corinthians, Galatians and Romans, insists upon a metahistory alternative to that of the Western Empire,

Paul differs significantly from certain postcolonial writers who
repudiate any and all metanarratives. The major way in which
Paul differs from most intellectuals of any age, of course, is that
his primary concern is to organize a movement of new communities who identified with the alternative history he presented.

Third, in anticipation of the imperial regime's restoration of
the Judean ruling class (roughly in 540 BCE), yet considering their
impotence in the larger imperial order, the prophetic visionary
who wrote the Servant Songs (Isa. 42.1-7; 49.1-6) envisaged a
paradigmatic world-historical role for tiny Israel in embodying justice as an example to benefit other peoples. As indicated already
in connection with Mark's Gospel above, the movement(s) that
Paul joined centuries later, apparently from its origins in Jesus'
Galilean mission, was inclusive of a diversity of people across
rulers' territorial boundaries. Soon after a community was established in Jerusalem, following Jesus' crucifixion, numbers of
Greek-speaking Jews from the diaspora joined, and carried the
message and movement into their own 'homes' in the Jewish
diaspora. Paul's initial mission field was Arabia, then with Barnabas and others, 'the regions of Syria and Cilicia'. There seems to
have been no disagreement over the movement's inclusion of
other peoples (better translation of *ethnē* than the essentialist
'Gentiles' and the modern 'nations'). Perhaps the leaders of the
early Jesus movement have a vision similar to that of recent Latin
American and Caribbean writers, in which 'Caliban' understands
his own history as an aspect of the history of all subject people
(Retamar 1989: 14; Said 1994: 214). Peter and James had no disagreement with Paul and Barnabas over the inclusion of other
peoples in the movement that embodied the fulfilment of the
promises to Abraham. 'There is no longer Jew or Greek... slave or
free... male and female' was the formal pronouncement at the
rite of entrance into the body politic (Gal. 3.28). This practice
carries into 'community organizing' an inclusiveness and diversity
that resembles recent decolonizing resistance literature, a
'pull... toward a more integrative view of human community and
human liberation' (Said 1994: 216).

It was Paul, however, the apostle with roots and experience in
the broader imperial culture, rather than James and Peter, the
peasant-fisherfolk from Galilee relocated to the Judean capital,

who pushed this 'more integrative view of human community and human liberation' into an 'international' movement planted more widely around the Empire it aimed to displace. He did not launch his own independent mission to the 'peoples' until more than 14 years after his commissioning as an envoy of Christ (Gal. 2.1). It seems likely, therefore, that only gradually and well after his inaugural 'revelation' did it become clear that his particular mission field among the 'uncircumcised' was to be the peoples in Asia Minor and Greece (and eventually Spain). Sharp disagreements then came to a head between Paul and other activists in the movement regarding the basis on which other peoples were to be incorporated into the movement, as evident particularly in his epistle to the Galatians. The 'Judaizers' against whom he vents such vitriol in Galatians insisted that to be included in the movement other peoples had, in effect, to join Israel, that is by the males undergoing the rite of circumcision, the mark of the covenant people. Paul, on the other hand, insists that other peoples can become members of the movement in their own right, as Galatians, Philippians and so on. Now that the promise to Abraham has been fulfilled in his seed, Christ, those who belong to Christ ('Jew or Greek') have become heirs of the promise (Gal. 3–4). Paul's politico-cultural agenda was complex. Over against the Roman imperial order he proclaimed to other subject peoples in the Eastern Mediterranean that history, which had all along been moving through Israel, not Rome, was now fulfilled in Christ's crucifixion and exaltation and an alternative society inaugurated. Yet Israel/Jews and Jewish cultural identity held no privilege in the new order; rather all were one, on the basis of whatever their previous 'ethnic' identity or social status. Although he privileged Israel's history, he gave no special status to Israelite identity. It was not necessary for non-Israelites to take on a distinctively Israelite identity. Again we may discern similarities to recent decolonizing writers, who, while rooted in a particular (new) nation, move beyond separatist or chauvinist concerns to ideas of 'community *among* cultures, peoples, and societies' (Said 1994: 217; Davidson 1978: 204).

The most significant way in which a postcolonial reading of Paul disrupts the standard essentialist, individualistic and depoliticized Augustinian-Lutheran Paul, consists in the rediscovery of the anti-imperial stance and program evident in his letters—for those with 'eyes to see'. For his discourse about Christ, Paul has invaded the very emperor cult by which imperial power relations were constituted in the cities such as Corinth and Ephesus, the two metropolitan bases from which he staged his mission in the provinces of Achaia and Asia. Some of the most basic symbols of his discourse, including 'gospel' itself, 'Savior/salvation', the *parousia* and 'faith', he took, almost certainly on purpose, directly from the emperor cult (Georgi 1991), which, like Christmas in the United States, simply pervaded the public space in the form of festivals, temples, shrines, inscriptions and ubiquitous images (Price 1984; Horsley 1997). The true Lord (the true emperor of the world), Jesus Christ, has been enthroned in heaven and is imminently to return to earth in a dramatic *parousia*, as when the emperor pays a state visit to a city, at which point Roman imperial rule will be finally terminated (1 Thess. 2.19; 3.13; 4.14-18; 5.23; 1 Cor. 15.23). 'The rulers of this age' in fact doomed themselves when, in their typical exercise of intimidating terrorizing violence, they 'crucified the Lord of glory', thus implementing the apocalyptic plan ('mystery') of God (1 Cor. 2.7-8). Paul has combined key imperial language with his Jewish apocalyptic discourse in an uncompromising opposition to the imperial order.

Perhaps the clearest indication of Paul's that the Roman imperial order stands under divine condemnation (and imminent termination!) while he and his movement already live under a new government or polity comes in Phil. 3.20-21:

> But our government/constitution [*politeuma*] is in heaven, and it is from there that we are expecting a Savior, the Lord Jesus Christ. He will transform the body of our humiliation that it may be conformed to the body of his glory, by the power that also enables him to make all things subject to himself.

That is indeed an apocalyptic statement, but contrary to the depoliticization of apocalypticism by Western biblical scholarship, it is also thereby a thoroughly political statement. The fact cannot be avoided that the context was the Roman Empire. According to the imperial ideology (or 'gospel'), Jupiter/Zeus and the other gods had given over all their power to Augustus (and his successors), who in establishing 'Peace and Security' (cf. 1 Thess. 5.3!) had become the Savior of the world. Paul stands diametrically opposed to the imperial order and ideology. The true God has certainly not given over power to the Roman emperor. Just the opposite: in the Christ events God is accomplishing the termination of the Roman imperial order. According to his counter-imperial 'gospel', while he and the 'assemblies' of his movement remain in the imperial order, *their* government is in heaven, from which the true, counter-emperor/Savior is soon to come. Meanwhile, known only to the movement, it is Christ who has been invested with power by God to subject all things to himself.

How seriously Paul took this counter-imperial 'gospel' of the counter-imperial 'Savior' and the counter-imperial 'government' is indicated in his almost obsessive 'building' of 'assemblies' and his instructions to them on their relations with 'the world'. Paul was more of an activist movement-builder than an intellectual. Indeed, his writings were means to 'edify' his 'assemblies', attempts to reinforce their solidarity amidst a hostile imperial environment (see esp. 1 Thess. and Phil.) In response to the many difficulties he found in the Corinthian community—some of which may have resulted from his own stubborn behavior—he indicates the degree to which he understood the 'assemblies' as, in effect, an alternative society.[3] The metropolitan context, particularly in Corinth, was a highly diverse mixture of often deracinated individuals cut loose from traditional social connections of family, lineage, *ethnos*, or village community. A metropolitan 'melting pot', except that new forms of social relations, hierarchical networks of patron–client relations, or trade, associations, or simply crowded living conditions, all in the public space pervaded by the imperial 'presence' established there by the provincial elite. Since Paul and his 'assemblies' lived in the 'world' and since they were aiming to bring more people into their own body politic, they were to have open dealings with other people in the society. Within their own community, however, they were to maintain strict ethical discipline (1 Cor. 5). As an almost self-sufficient community themselves, with their own 'government' in heaven, they were to handle their own internal conflicts, and by no means to resort to the official courts (1 Cor. 6.1-8). Most surprising of all

3. For expansion of such reflections on Paul's agenda based on exegesis of 1 Corinthians and related passages in Paul's other letters, see Horsley 1998.

to 'enlightened' Western theologians, perhaps, is Paul's adamant opposition to 'eating food offered to idols' in temple-banquets. After all, he ostensibly agreed with the enlightened Corinthian 'spiritual' that 'no idol/god in the world really exists' (1 Cor. 8.4). In the ensuing statement, almost an aside, however, Paul rejects this 'enlightened' theology: '—in fact there are many gods and many lords'! In their enlightenment and depoliticization of Paul as 'religious', moreover, enlightened Western theologians misunderstood the significance of 'sacrifices', or those silly ritual meals. In Greco-Roman antiquity as elsewhere in world history, such ritual meals constituted the networks that formed the very fabric of society, from household and lineage to city state to imperial power relations (Stowers 1995). That is why Paul was so adamantly opposed to 'idolatry' (including partaking in such meals) and insisted on the absolute mutual exclusivity of 'partaking in the table of the Lord' and 'partaking in the table of demons'. But it is impossible to separate the political from the religious solidarity of those mutually exclusive communities. That is Paul's recognition and that is his point in 1 Cor. 8-10. Temporarily they were still living within the 'present form of this world', which was 'passing away' (1 Cor. 7.31). But they were already to constitute an alternative society, open to recruiting others, yet in every significant way embodying a new social order ('no longer...').

These latter two aspects discerned in a postcolonial reading of Paul, his adamant uncompromising opposition to the Roman imperial order and his formation of communities as a kind of international anti-imperial alternative society, may be causes for reflection in the current postcolonial context. It is impossible to separate Paul's rhetorical-cultural opposition from his active political opposition to it—to the point of devoting all his obsessive energy to building an alternative society. In modern Western society, culture and politic-economy have been separated. To the extent that our postcolonial activity, like 'decolonizing cultural resistance' (Said's phrase), is primarily cultural, without political engagement, we acquiesce in this Western fragmentation of our lives. Yet even if we accept confinement to the cultural sphere, postcolonial criticism has political significance one way or another. The postcolonial critics mentioned at the outset raise questions about the relationship between postcolonial discourse and the reconfiguration of earlier forms of domination in the neo-imperialism of global capital.

In this connection, Paul's adamant opposition to the Roman imperial order is suggestive, once we recognize what was involved. As Roman imperialism broke down subject people's indigenous culture and social forms and imposed forms of 'civilization', the form of imperial power relations shifted from application of military violence to socio-economic networks of patronage and the religious festivals, shrines, and images of the imperial cult (Price 1984; Chow 1992; Horsley 1997). No army and no elaborate imperial political administration was necessary. In the Greek world where Paul focused his mission, in such cities as Corinth and Ephesus, imperial power relations were *constituted* by patronage networks and the imperial cult, with heavy reliance on *images* that embodied the imperial 'presence' in public space and private awareness. Since the apex of imperial power relations was made 'present' in the far reaches of the Empire, however, what they opposed was readily evident to Paul and others who wanted to resist. The neo-imperialism of global capital also relies heavily on cultural forms to constitute the power relations through which it exploits labor and markets products. Very little actual exercise of military power is necessary and politics are used mainly to maintain 'peace and security', the context of productivity and marketing. As in the Roman Principate, 'images' are the key, substituting more and more for metanarrative. Unlike the Roman imperial order, however, global capital hides behind the images, unnoticed by unaware people. And unlike the centralization of the network of Roman imperial power, the power relations of global capital are decentralized. Indeed, decentralized global capital can even use multiculturalism to advantage in marketing products through manipulation of images behind which it hides.

Paul attempted to build an international movement of alternative communities as well as to articulate an alternative metahistory in resistance to the Roman imperial order. It is difficult to discern what, on the threshold of the twenty-first century, might hold promise for even an alternative history, let alone for an international movement of resistance. But postcolonial discourse will at least help loosen the grip by which Western cultural disciplines hold our intellectual practices in their preferred patterns. Insofar

as postcolonial intellectuals identify with the subordinate everywhere and make alliances with feminists and minority interests in
the West/North in common disruption of current cultural hege-
monies and relations of domination, they may also form networks
if not movements of resistance to the forces that hide behind
neoimperial production of images. At least postcolonial intellectuals can develop representations in biblical studies that are
emancipatory in their effects and can provide a basis for political
challenges to regnant forms of domination.

BIBLIOGRAPHY

Ahmad Aijaz
       1992   *In Theory: Classes, Nations, Literatures* (London: Verso).
Anderson, Benedict
       1991   *Imagined Communities: Reflections on the Origin and Spread of National-
                   ism* (London: Verso, rev. edn).
Chow, John K.
       1992   *Patronage and Power* (Sheffield: JSOT Press).
Coronil, Fernando
       1992   'Can Postcoloniality Be Decolonized? Imperial Banality and Post-
                   colonial Power', *Public Culture* 5: 99-100.
Davidson, Basil
       1978   *Africa in Modern History: The Search for a New Society* (London: Allen
                   Lane).
Dirlik, Arif
       1994   'The Postcolonial Aura: Third World Criticism and the Age of
                   Global Capitalism', *Critical Inquiry* 20: 328-56.
Georgi, Dieter
       1991   *Theocracy in Paul's Praxis and Theology* (Minneapolis: Fortress Press).
Horsley, Richard A.
       1995   *Galilee: History, Politics, People* (Valley Forge, PA: Trinity Press Inter-
                   national).
       1998   *1 Corinthians* (Abingdon New Testament Commentaries; Nashville:
                   Abingdon Press).
Horsley, Richard A. (ed.)
       1997   *Paul and Empire: Religion and Power in Roman Imperial Society* (Valley
                   Forge, PA: Trinity Press International).
Kelber, Werner
       1974   *The Kingdom in Mark: A New Place and a New Time* (Philadelphia:
                   Fortress Press).
Kwok, Pui-lan
       1993   'Discovering the Bible in the Nonbiblical World', *Semeia* 47 (1989):
                   25-42; repr. in N. Gottwald and R. Horsley (eds.), *The Bible and
                   Liberation: Political and Social Hermeneutics* (Maryknoll, NY: Orbis
                   Books, rev. edn): 17-30.

Mosala, Itumeleng J.
    1989   *Biblical Hermeneutics and Black Theology in South Africa* (Grand Rapids, MI: Eerdmans).

Prakash, Gyan
    1992   'Postcolonial Criticism and Indian Historiography', *Social Text* 31 (32): 8-19.

Price, S.R.F.
    1984   *Rituals and Power: The Roman Imperial Cult in Asia Minor* (Cambridge: Cambridge University Press).

Retamar, Roberto Fernandez
    1989   *Caliban and Other Essays* (Minneapolis: University of Minnesota Press).

Said, Edward W.
    1985   *Orientalism* (London: Penguin Books [1978])
    1994   *Culture and Imperialism* (New York: Vintage).

Scott, James C.
    1977   'Protest and Profanation: Agrarian Revolt and the Little Tradition', *Theory and Society* 4: 1-38, 211-46.

Shohat, Ella
    1992   'Notes on the "Post-Colonial"', *Social Text* 31 (32): 99-113.

Stowers, Stanley K.
    1995   'Greeks Who Sacrifice and Those Who Do Not: Toward an Anthropology of Greek Religion', in L.M. White and L. Yarbrough, *The Social World of the First Christians: Essays in Honor of Wayne Meeks* (Minneapolis: Fortress Press): 293-333.

Weems, Renita
    1991   'Reading her way Through the Struggle: African American Women and the Bible', in Cain Hope Felder (ed.), *Stony the Road We Trod: African American Biblical Interpretation* (Minneapolis: Fortress Press): 57-77.

PART IV

NARRATIVAL REFIGURATIONS

On Color-Coding Jesus:
An Interview with Kwok Pui-lan

KWOK PUI-LAN

> *Our Father* **in the heavens,**
> your name be revered.
> Impose your imperial rule,
> **enact your will on earth as you have in heaven.**
> Provide us with the bread we need for the day.
> Forgive our debts
> to the extent that we have forgiven those in debt to us.
> AND PLEASE DON'T SUBJECT US TO TEST AFTER TEST,
> **but rescue us from the evil one.**

Quest: Why are you obsessed with Jesus?
Kwok: I am not obsessed with Jesus, but I am obsessed with other people's obsession with Jesus.
Quest: Why?
Kwok: When people in Europe were obsessed with the historical Jesus in the nineteenth century, the whole world was in trouble. Nowadays, many people in North America are obsessed with the newest quest for Jesus. I am concerned with the social symptoms that make such a quest so popular and the wider implications for the rest of the world.
Quest: Why is the Lord's Prayer marked with different colors?
Kwok: Since 1985, a group of mostly Euro-American scholars have formed the Jesus Seminar and met regularly to determine who Jesus really was and what he actually said. They used red to indicate those sayings that are close to what Jesus actually said, pink for the words less certain, gray for the ideas close to his own, and black for words created by his followers or borrowed from common lore.[1] In the book *The Five Gospels* published by the Sem-

---

1.   Red = italic, black = bold, pink = underlined, gray = small capitals.

inar, the Lord's Prayer in Mt. 6.9-13 was color-coded as shown. As you can imagine, feminists are enraged to know that Jesus only said 'our Father' and the blacks are furious that those words that Jesus did not actually say are coded black.

Quest: Are they serious about this color-coding business? It seems very arbitrary to me.

Kwok: The fact that they are still casting colored balls in this electronic age is quite funny, but they are dead serious about their work. The Jesus Seminar has been billed as the first interdisciplinary quest for Jesus, and not simply a historical quest. Furthermore, the newest quest has caught the attention of the mass media, and been reported on National Public Radio, in *People* magazine and *Time*. In November 1996, a TV station sent a crew to cover the Jesus Seminar during the annual meeting of the Society of Biblical Literature in New Orleans. The program was aired around Christmas time in 1996 and repeated during Easter in 1997. The quest books are very popular too. John Dominic Crossan's *The Historical Jesus* reportedly sold more than 50,000 copies within two years, and there are many popular versions of this newest research. The Trinity Institute in New York organized the Jesus 2000 seminar in 1996 with many people linked up through satellite in churches and universities across the United States. Many people listened to the discussion and called in to ask questions. The quest has indeed become a cultural phenomenon.

Quest: What do you see as the significance of such a phenomenon?

Kwok: Isn't it interesting that the quests are always located in Europe and North America? I have not seen such obsession in Asia, Africa, Latin America, or the Caribbean. People living outside the metropolitan centers do not seem to be terribly concerned with the quest. Some African Christians have even said: 'We do not need to quest for Jesus, we have never lost him.' I have also observed that the first quest took place in Europe when the colonization of the world was at its zenith. Today, the United States has become the only Superpower and the newest quest has caught the popular imagination. Do you think this is mere coincidence?

Quest: It sounds like you are getting at something important, can you say a bit more?

Kwok: The quest for Jesus is a quest for origins. I am fascinated by this constant need to search for origins. What are they searching for? What is the lack, as Lacan may have asked? What are the functions the quest serves and who are the people it benefits? I think the quest for Jesus is a coded form of the search for white male identity. In the nineteenth century, Europe underwent tremendous cultural and political changes as the colonizers were confronted by the colonized in many parts of the world. The first quest could not have taken place without the new knowledge brought to the metropolitan centers about the myths, cultures, and religions of the colonized people. In a forthcoming essay I have argued that the search for Jesus must be read against the search for 'natives' to conquer and subdue. The encounter with the 'natives' created anxiety and necessitated the quest for self-identity. The epistemological framework of the first quest was constructed out of a combination of Orientalist philology, racist ideology, and Eurocentric study of other people's mythology and religions.

Quest: That's strange. I thought the historical quest was a scientific and objective study of the Bible, challenging the doctrinal authority of the church.

Kwok: For a long time I was taught to read the historical quest in that way. But I have come to see that that was basically a European script. Where in the Third World did you see people using the historical quest to challenge the church, except maybe in very tiny academic enclaves?

Quest: Then why do the Americans have to search for origins?

Kwok: The straight white males in America have made a lot of noises saying that they have lost a lot of ground to women, minorities, and gays and lesbians. The mass media in the US has played up the angry white male syndrome. Whenever the white males are not certain about their identity, they search for Jesus.

Quest: Is it very much like a myth of origin?

Kwok: Precisely. As Foucault has shown in his genealogical method, an 'origin' or a 'starting point' is culturally and discursively constructed in order to establish some sort of lineage: new and old, continuity or discontinuity, and resemblance and difference. It is never value-neutral because the question of 'origin' is always enmeshed in the systems of discourse and is imbued with the issue of power. We have heard it many times before: What is the origin of the Aryan race? What is the origin of the Indo-European languages? What is the origin of foot-binding? What is the origin of Islam? What is the origin of all these dark-pigmented people in London, New York, and Amsterdam?

Quest: And they have even established a genealogy for the different quests for the historical Jesus.

Kwok: I think you are absolutely right. Now you cannot study Jesus without having a road map: the first quest, the second quest, the third quest, the new quest, the newest quest, the historical quest, the interdisciplinary quest, the Jewish quest, the German quest, the French quest, the American quest, and so forth. You need to know when it all started, how one quest is different from the other quests, and who are the 'seminal' thinkers of each of the quests. They created a classification system and myths of the beginnings and the ends. This is how a whole discipline came into being and, once it was established, how it performed its disciplinary function of excluding all other discourses, dismissing them as unscholarly and non-academic.

Quest: You say that the nineteenth-century white males were threatened by the encounter with the natives. Who are twentieth-century American white males threatened by?

Kwok: The answer is pretty simple. You just have to open any daily newspaper or turn on the TV. They are threatened by the illegal immigrant, the welfare queen, the pregnant teenager, the rapist on the street, the child molester, the angry blacks, the suicidal youth, the outspoken Indian, the women who ask for abortion, the rich black man who kills his white wife, the Unibomber, the militia, the lawyer, the doctor, the insurance agent, the woman who kills her two sons, the judge who decides divorce settlements, and so forth. That these people make 'news' almost every other day tells you something about the psyche of the people who manufacture such 'news' and those who consume it.

Quest: What have all these people to do with the quest for Jesus?

Kwok: The white world is not the same as before, or is it? For many white folks, the world they are used to is not there anymore. There is no melting pot to melt things, and there is no consensus of what they want people to assimilate into. People debate about the literary canon to teach the kids, about whether to distribute condoms at schools, about affirmative action policies, about the rights of legal immigrants, and about protecting the borders. The Catholic Church is constantly pushed to ordain women and married men. The Protestant mainline denominations are busy talking about whether to ordain gays and lesbians as priests and whether non-married clergy should be celibate. The Catholics, the Protestant denominations and the evangelicals are all in the same boat of having to deal with cases of sexual abuse committed by the clergy.

Quest: It really looks like things are falling apart.

Kwok: Well, when have things been together? Just a generation ago, the black kids and the white kids could not study in the same school or swim in the same pool!

Quest: So are you saying that this is the cultural matrix from which the quest of Jesus emerged.

Kwok: Yes, I think the changing political and cultural landscape of the US has much to do with the popular attention given to the Jesus research these days. If the quest for Jesus went hand in hand with the quest for 'natives' in the nineteenth century, the 'natives' are already inside the US today, and the whites do not need to go out to find them. In fact, they don't know how to deal with them or get rid of them.

Quest: That is quite a contrast.

Kwok: The other day I was reading the *New York Times Book Review*, which is a very interesting cultural artifact, as you know. The non-fiction section is particularly illuminating. The first book review was on a biography of Charlie Chaplin, followed by a review of Alan Dershowitz's latest book *The Vanishing American Jew*. The subtitle of this book is very telling: *In Search of Jewish Identity for the Next Century*. Then comes a review of Keith Richburg's *Out of America*. Richburg is an African American journalist and the memoir talks about his sojourn in Africa, covering news for the *Washington Post*. He went to Africa to escape America's race wars, but could hardly find Africa home. There was a review of a book about the last secret of the Vietnam War, a nightmare that continues to haunt the American psyche. Other books reviewed include a story about a woman having an incestuous affair with her father, and poems and prose from India. Another piece is a review of *The Idea of Decline in Western History*. The fiction section is also very enticing. It includes reviews of a book by a gay writer, David Leavitt, a fiction about several wandering emigrants, and a novel set in Martinique in the Caribbean. The cover of the *Book Review* portrays a brown-skinned Caribbean woman and the back of a fair-skinned man who is probably gazing at the woman.

Quest: I wish I had read that issue. It must be very eye opening.

Kwok: Indeed. An idea suddenly dawned on me while reading the review: the newest quest of Jesus in America is simultaneously a quest for the Jews, the blacks, the gays, the dangerous women, the immigrants, the Indians, the women with brown skin, the loss, the decline...

Quest: Are you finding anything interesting in the newest quest that addresses this situation?

Kwok: Oh, many interesting things. For example, I am fascinated by people's fascination with Q, the source of Jesus' sayings. It is intriguing that Burton Mack's book is called *The Lost Gospel: The Book of Q and Christian Origins*. Something has been lost, and found again. Amazing! Mack tells us the people of Q were not interested in Jesus as a messiah or the Christ because they did not say much about his death and resurrection. They thought of him as a guru whose teaching helped them to live in troubled times. Well, I have seen some of the latter-day New Age gurus on TV. A popular one is Deepak Chopra, a medical doctor who can recycle Hinduism for his modern-day audiences. He can come up with some nice titles for his books, like *Ageless Body, Timeless Mind; Boundless Energy;* and *Restful Sleep*. His books and health programs have earned him millions in the past two years. It's comforting to know that Christian scholars have found ancient wisdom sayings in the Christian tradition, so that people do not need to find them in foreign lands. Hopefully, the Christian Q is less expensive.

Quest: Are there other titles that are worth noting?

Kwok: How about Marcus Borg's *Meeting Jesus Again for the First Time*? 'Again' for the 'first time', Borg is almost pleading here. He touches on a raw nerve, that many people in the US do not know much about Jesus and many simply dismiss him as irrelevant. Borg lifts up the images of Jesus as a Spirit-filled person, a 'holy person' or healer, to help his modern readers to understand who Jesus was. Healing, of course, has a lot of currency in the self-help books, and the American people have a craving for spirituality, if not institutionalized religion. Everyone wants and desires to be a Spirit-filled person these days.

Quest: What about Crossan's *The Historical Jesus?*

Kwok: We certainly should not leave out this one, a book of such weight. The subtitle is *The Life of a Mediterranean Jewish Peasant.* A peasant—how romantic! Have you read the book? Its beginning is really charming:

> In the beginning was the performance; not the word alone, not the deed alone, but both, each indelibly marked with the other forever. He comes as yet unknown into a hamlet of Lower Galilee. He is watched by the cold hard eyes of peasants living long enough at subsistence level to know exactly where the line is drawn between poverty and destitution. He looks like a beggar, yet his eyes lack the proper cringe, his voice the proper whine, his walk the proper shuffle. He speaks about the rule of God, and they listen as much from curiosity as anything else.

Is this Jesus? In another age he would be called a 'primitive' and a Lévi-Strauss would have rushed to dissect how his savage mind worked.

Quest: But isn't the book a serious reconstruction of who Jesus was, what he did, and what he said?

Kwok: Indeed, the book pays attention to minute details as if conducting warfare or a chess game. Crossan says in the prologue that his methodology has a triple triadic process: the campaign, the strategy and the tactics. Accusing others of engaging in textual or cultural looting, he says he is committed to the regimen of a strict scientific stratigraphy. He disarms the suspicion of the readers by saying in the beginning that his methodology does not claim a spurious objectivity. He declares that he is concerned not with an unattainable objectivity, but with an attainable honesty. A very smart move! The book is very dense. It is divided into three parts, and the titles of these parts really open the American mind. No wonder the book is selling so well!

Quest: What are these titles?

Kwok: 'Brokered Empire', 'Embattled Brokerage' and 'Brokerless Kingdom'. Aren't they well chosen?

Quest: What about the content?

Kwok: Very well written. The subheadings are just terrific: 'A Friendly Sea in a Hostile Landscape', 'Against the Britons and the Asians', 'The Frog-Prince's Passion for Trade', 'Free under Father Zeus', 'I Cannot Conceal my Private Sentiments', 'A King without a Dynasty', 'Native Revolt against Rome', 'Children and Disciples Complain', 'Against the Patriarchal Family', 'The Message of an Open Secret', 'Do This in Memory of Me'. These could easily be the chapters of an American novel that would surely hit the *New York Times* bestseller list.

Quest: Are women involved in the quest at all?

Kwok: Who are the women you are talking about? The white women? Well, a few participate in the Jesus seminar, but I don't think white women in general are as excited as the white men. The white women are not obsessed with the origin, they are obsessed with whether Jesus the Messiah was male and female, and whether the gender of the savior made any difference.

Quest: Do you think the newest quest can shed light on this?

Kwok: Jesus has many identities in the newest quest: a political revolutionary, a magician, a Galilean charismatic, a rabbi, a proto-Pharisee, an Essene, an eschatological prophet, a healer, a sage, and so on. I assume these are gender-inclusive descriptions. But nobody has yet discovered that Jesus was a woman. I hope some white women may find *The Lost Gospel: The Book of F*. If white men can discover Q, why can't their female counterparts discover F, for 'Fräulein', 'femme' and 'feminine'?

Quest: There exists the *Gospel of Mary*, right?

Kwok: Precisely. There may be other works in this genre, say the *Gospel of Sophia*, the *Gospel of Joanna* and the *Gospel of Susanna*. And they may help women to discover the *Book of F*. With luck, a wandering shepherd may discover a jar and find something like the Dead Sea Scrolls or the Nag Hammadi texts. Whenever new texts were 'found' and brought to the attention of the metropolitan centers, the search for origins began again and a new discipline evolved. First, the Europeans 'discovered' the sacred books, the *Gita*, the *Golden Bough*, the *Lotus Sutra*, the *Dao de jing* and the *Gospel of Thomas*. Then came the Indologist, the Sinologist, the Sanskritist, the Orientalist, the philologist, the historian of religions, the Hinduist, the Buddhologist and the Gnosticist.

Quest: What about those traditions that have no texts?

Kwok: They were studied by other experts: the anthropologist, the ethnographer, the primitivist, the sociologist, the structuralist, the linguist, the comparativist and the masters of savage minds.

Quest: How did the study of other religions influence the study of the Bible?

Kwok: A lot. The Europeans treated the sacred books of the East as *fetishes*, just as they have treated the charms, amulets, baskets, bridal dresses, bones, arrows and feathers of other cultures. Having admired and displayed these newly discovered texts in their libraries and museums, they were eager to use the same techniques to fetishize the Bible, which of course, was an 'Oriental' document. The missionaries helped in the global fetishization process by taking the Bible all over the world. The Bible has been imbued with magical power because it is considered the Word of God.

Quest: What makes you think the Bible was rendered as a fetish?

Kwok: I was reading how the Europeans and Euro-Americans have studied and re-presented the Native American, African and Asian religious traditions. Suddenly I became aware that the manuscripts, the papyrus, the scrolls and the blockprints were treated in similar ways as the bones, the stones, the necklaces and the charms. They have to be collected, dissected, stratified, classified, coded and then displayed. You can see all these objects in the British Museum, only that they are in different rooms. Fetishization was the dominant mode of desiring, acquiring, and collecting other people's sacred objects. The drive to fetishize unavoidably shaped European and Euro-American attitudes toward their 'own' sacred objects, including the Bible.

Quest: How so?

Kwok: Let me use the study of Buddhism in the West as an example. Have you read the magnificent book *Curators of the Buddha*? In some ways, *Curators of the Buddha* is a belated response to Said's *Orientalism*. Applying postcolonial theories to the study of Buddhism, the book traces the intricate relation between Buddhist Studies in Europe and North America and colonialism. The introduction to the book explains how Buddhism was constituted as a body of texts to be studied and analyzed by scholars in Western libraries who really did not need to travel to Buddhist Asia. The texts constituted for the scholars the 'golden', 'classical', 'original', 'primitive' or 'pure' Buddhism. These texts told us what the Buddha had taught and represented the authentic dharma against which all Buddhist cultures in the course of history were to be judged. This 'classical' or 'primitive' Buddhism, of course, was a creation of Europe and controlled by the experts. These experts were and still are too busy studying the dead languages of Pali, Sanskrit and 'classical' Chinese to pay attention to how these texts are interpreted by Buddhists in Asia.

Quest: So they study the classical texts as if they were fossils and museum objects.

Kwok: Yes, and what makes you think they would study the Bible differently? Where can you go to in Europe and North America to study the Bible as a living book and not just as ancient texts of a classical age long gone?

Quest: No wonder scholars talk about the excavation of archaeological and textual sites.

Kwok: Indeed. Remember Crossan talks about inventory, stratification, attestation, first stratum, second stratum, third stratum, fourth stratum and the sequence of strata? All this meticulous digging, brushing, separating, differentiating and labelling will help us find the man who was long dead: Jesus of Nazareth. It is a pity they can only find the texts but not the bones.

Quest: Why do you pay so much attention to how the Europeans and Euro-Americans are searching for Jesus? Is postcolonial criticism just a negation of the West?

Kwok: I know where your question is coming from. Edward Said and Gayatri Chakravorty Spivak have been asked similar questions too. When Said was speaking in Palestine, some of the people there were talking about the West and 'the rest of us' and Said lost his temper. He retorted that no one can cut himself off from his own past, so one's experience is necessarily heterogeneous. He said it is futile for those of us who have been colonized to try to recover some primitive, unalloyed pure essence that has not been defiled or corrupted. You think we should start the quest for the original or authentic Chinese, Nigerian or Brazilian?

Quest: No, I don't mean that.

Kwok: I was born in the British Colony of Hong Kong and I was overdetermined and multiply inscribed without my choosing.

Many postcolonial intellectuals, whether living in their own countries or in a diaspora, share my experience of having to negotiate
daily multiple identities, cultural worlds, and languages and
dialects.

Quest: So there is no simple answer to where the colonial world
ends and where the colonized world begins?

Kwok: Yes, our whole conversation has really shown that the
metropolitan centers were as deeply inscribed, corrupted and pol-
luted, if you will, by the imperializing process as the colonized. A
gaze at the Other is simultaneously a gaze at yourself. I agree with
Stuart Hall when he says that postcolonial discourse has helped us
question the binary construction of here/there, colonizer/colo-
nized, inside/outside, home/abroad, and then/now. Hall is right
to observe that colonization is an essentially transcultural and
transnational 'global' process. We have to begin to question the
naive and simplistic construction of inside/outside of the colonial
system in order to understand the multidimensional ways that the
colonizer/colonized reorganize and restratify one another. The
various quests have always been analyzed and classified according
to the tune of European or North American imperial grand narratives. Now we have to rewrite the history from the decentered,
diasporic, Third World, Jewish, black, gay and lesbian, immigrant,
brown-skinned women's perspectives, since the quest for Jesus is
also a quest for us. We have authorized the quest, though we have
seldom claimed it.

Quest: I have never thought of that.

Kwok: The rewriting helps us to liberate ourselves from the spells
of European and Euro-American hallucinations that haunt our
minds. These voices are especially strong in the academic study of
Jesus today. Without clearing our minds, we can hardly hear other
voices, our own and others'.

Quest: Then we can hear how contemporary Christians from all
over the world are talking about Jesus.

Kwok: Instead of treating the Bible as a fetish, we must reimagine
it as *diasporic adventure*. I was fascinated by Adam Phillips's insight
in *Terrors and Experts* that the opposite of a fetish is an adventure.
What do you think of that? The fragments, papyrus, manuscripts
and codices of the Bible from the wilderness in Palestine and
Egypt ended up in the museums and libraries in Europe and the

US. Isn't that an adventure? There is another parallel process whereby the Bible was brought from the metropolitan centers to Jamaica, Sri Lanka, Kenya and the whole world. The Bible learned to speak different languages and dialects on the way. Can you guess how many different names Jesus has in the world?

Quest: I don't know. How many are there?

Kwok: No one knows for sure. The Bible, as Northrop Frye says, is a great code, and we learn a lot about color-coding if we are not color-blind. There are more postcolonial readings of the Bible these days, and the global recoding process has begun. It is going to be fascinating.

Quest: Indeed, I just can't wait to begin my own quest now.

WORKS TO ASSIST FURTHER QUESTS

Borg, Marcus J.
   1994   *Jesus in Contemporary Scholarship* (Valley Forge, PA: Trinity Press
            International).
Buttigieg, Joseph A., and Paul A. Bové
   1993   'An Interview with Edward W. Said', *Boundary* 2 (20): 1-25.
Crossan, John Dominic
   1991   *The Historical Jesus: The Life of a Mediterranean Jewish Peasant* (San
            Francisco: Harper San Francisco).
Frye, Northrop
   1982   *The Great Code: The Bible and Literature* (New York: Harcourt Brace
            Jovanovich).
Funk, Robert W., Roy W. Hoover and the Jesus Seminar
   1993   *The Five Gospels: The Search for the Authentic Words of Jesus* (New York:
            Macmillan).
Gospel of F
   (To be found)
Hall, Stuart
   1996   'When Was "the Post-Colonial"? Thinking at the Limit', in Iain
            Chambers and Lidia Curti (eds.), *The Post-Colonial Question: Common
            Skies, Divided Horizons* (New York: Routledge & Kegan Paul): 242-60.
Kwok, Pui-lan
   1995   *Discovering the Bible in the Non-Biblical World* (Maryknoll, NY: Orbis
            Books).
   forthcoming 'Jesus/The Native: Biblical Studies from a Postcolonial Perspective',
            in Fernando F. Segovia and Mary Ann Tolbert (eds.), *Teaching the
            Bible: Discourses and Politics of Biblical Pedagogy*.
Lopez, Donald S., Jr
   1995   *Curators of the Buddha: The Study of Buddhism under Colonialism*
            (Chicago: University of Chicago Press).

Mack, Burton L.
    1993   *The Lost Gospel: The Book of Q and Christian Origins* (San Francisco:
                Harper San Francisco).
New York Times Book Review
 1997 30 March
Phillips, Adam
    1995   *Terrors and Experts* (Cambridge, MA: Harvard University Press).

Experiences with a Biblical Story

BASTIAAN WIELENGA[1]

It was in the beginning of the 1960s, at the time of the old-colonial conflict between the Kingdom of the Netherlands and the Republic of Indonesia over West-Irian, which the Dutch had kept under their control after Indonesia had achieved its independence. An Indonesian student pastor, Siem, and I, both of us working in West Berlin, were invited by the SCM in that city to preach together at the annual World Day of Prayer of Students, while our countries were at war with each other. I don't remember whether the text was given to us or whether we had chosen it ourselves. It was the story of the encounter between the hostile brothers Jacob and Esau, as narrated in Genesis 32–33.

While studying the text together we made use of the German translation by Buber and Rosenzweig which differs from so many modern translations by its closeness to Hebrew language and style, repeating words of the same root which give clues to the understanding of particular texts and of wider connections throughout Scripture. A Dutch rabbi-like exegete, Breukelman, had introduced me and many others in the Dutch SCM to this way of listening to biblical texts.

The text narrates Jacob's preparations for handling the encounter with his brother whom he had cheated long before (32.3-21). Then we hear of his strange encounter at the crossing of the Jabbok (32.22-32) and it concludes with the actual encounter of the two brothers (33.1-11).

Historico-critical commentaries set apart the Peniel story and

1.   These reflections were written in honour of Christoph Hinz, a theologian who lived and worked in the GDR, who interpreted the Bible and contemporary developments in a mutually illuminating way.

usual sermon practice tends to do the same. But we found how
closely the stories are intertwined through several keywords. We
followed these hints given by R, who according to Buber/Rosen-
zweig, is more than a 'Redactor' or editor, and is, rather 'Rabbe-
nou', that is, 'our Rabbi', the one who teaches us through the text
in its final form.

Jacob cannot meet Esau face to face. He tries to hide himself
behind a present of herds of camels, asses and goats. Most translations obscure the point made by the narration in Hebrew:

> For he said to himself: I will cover his face with the present that
> goes before my face, afterwards I will see his face, maybe he lifts up
> my face (Gen. 32.20).

In the night a struggle takes place, as feared. But the adversary is
not Esau, out of whose hand Jacob had prayed to be 'delivered' by
God (32.11). It is God who appears at the side of Esau and con-
fronts Jacob with his past: 'What is your name?' God's face
assumes the features of the face of the brother.

> Jacob called the name of the place Peniel, face of God, because I
> have seen God, face to face and my life is delivered (32.30).

The sun rises, Esau comes, and Jacob sees in the friendly features
of the brother who embraces him the features of God. He insists
that Esau accepts his present,

> for truly to see your face is like seeing the face of God, with such
> favour have you received me (33.10).

And now the word 'present', used for the camels and goats, is
replaced by a keyword which is at the centre of the Jacob–Esau
story and connects it with the overall theme of the book of Genesis: blessing.

> Accept, I pray you, my blessing that is brought to you, because God
> has dealt graciously with me, and because I have enough (33.11).

Unfortunately, unlike the King James Version, the RSV and other
later translations do not have the word 'blessing'—they have
'gift'—so that we are not led to recall that the conflict between
Jacob and Esau had been exactly about the question who would
be the bearer of the blessing given to Abraham and Isaac. That
blessing had been reconfirmed to a limping Jacob at Peniel

(32.29), who now has come to understand that the blessing which he had tried to grab was meant to be shared.

As this story was told in Israel the listeners would associate the two brothers with the peoples of Israel and Edom who most of the time in Israel's history were in conflict with each other. So Siem and I heard in it a message showing our nations, in bloody conflict, the way to reconciliation. In the liberation struggles of the Third World, in the conflicts over the heritage of colonial empires, God appears on the side of the victims of deceit and monopolization and asks the nations which have become rich and powerful through colonialism about their past. The text calls them to discover the face of God in the angry critique of their colonial past. That past has to be faced and named, even if the names are as unwelcome as 'colonialism' or 'imperialism'. Repentance over what has been done since Columbus and Vasco da Gama five hundred years ago is the way to new, brotherly relationships.

A few years later I was invited to preach in the village in which I grew up during the Second World War. There was a growing polarization in Dutch society, including the churches, over the question of the apartheid regime in South Africa and resistance against it. I asked the congregation to try to look at what was happening from the perspective of the black brother who had been deceived, and to hear in the critique of the African National Congress, regarding the whole system of apartheid, God's critique of our past. As usual I had to conduct the evening service as well. The elder who was in charge confronted me a few minutes before the beginning of the service: what I had been preaching in the morning was wrong. The blacks were not our brothers, they were not humans like us. Would I allow my daughter to marry a black man? I was stunned: plain, hard-boiled racism from the mouth of a respected orthodox Reformed elder who throughout his life had attended church twice every Sunday, like his white Calvinist brothers in the land of apartheid. In this congregation I had learnt as a child to pray for prisoners in the concentration camps of the Nazis.

But obviously we have to go back further in history. This brother must have grown up with the same books which I also cherished as a boy, books in which the Boers were glorified as resistance fighters against the imperialist Britishers. That the same Boers, singing the same Psalms, fought against black Zulus and Bantus as conquerors and oppressors did not, for a long time, present itself as a problem to their Dutch fellow-believers.

All that came to mind much later. Stunned as I was I somehow got through the liturgy and the sermon. Afterwards the elder asked me why I had left out the Apostles' Creed. I had not done it on purpose—I simply forgot it. But it made sense as an act of omission, as I tried to explain, because his views about the blacks contradicted all the sentences of the creed which he found so important.

Working in India, the Jacob–Esau story became relevant to me again, disclosing other dimensions in connection with the problems of development and religion. It was the time of intensive debates about development. Aid money flowed. World Bank and World Council of Churches, technocrats and theologians competed in offering and propagating various concepts and projects. Of course, the ecumenical approach was much better. But even there seemed to be a reluctance to face a more radical analysis of the causes of poverty and of the problems of aid within the framework of a global and local economy geared to the logic of accumulation. The request of critical groups to spend more aid money on campaigns against multinational companies and in support of countries like Nicaragua in order to expose the powers of global capital was mostly being ignored. The more representatives of funding agencies turned up, the more their projects appeared to me like the herds of goats, sheep and camels behind which Jacob hid himself in the hope that his brother would forget how he had been deceived earlier, and would not notice that he was being deceived once again. In that connection I heard in the Marxist critique of capitalism, God's voice asking us about our name, in order to reveal the real game which is still being played. Its name is not development but accumulation, and thus exploitation.

One of the students with whom I read and discussed the story, listened to it with one of the great problems of Indian society in mind. Religion very often serves, in daily life, the purpose of securing divine blessings. That is equally true for Hindus, Christians and Muslims. It makes the business of religious rituals and prayers sometimes as off-putting as the story of Jacob's deceit. This student saw in Esau the secular sort of person who does not indulge in such practices. God appears on his side, and religious-minded people who appeal to God for protection and prosperity have to discover him as representative of God's forgiveness for the misunderstanding and misuse of his blessing.

One year later this student became assistant pastor in a parish of very poor hill people. His bishop insisted that the parish should contribute more to the treasury of the church. He should preach more forcefully about 'Christian giving'. He refused, and the bishop decided to increase the rent of the poor tenants occupying church land. The assistant pastor advised them to get legal protection against this measure of the bishop. He risked his ordination in a church in which absolute obedience is considered to be the highest virtue. Yet, the ordination did take place.

In the course of time I have related to other types of interpretation of the Jacob–Esau story. Some followers of Breukelman are inclined to despise all other methods and especially the approach of historico-critical exegesis. I have learnt from my mentor friend Christopher Hinz—the East-German theologian to whom this essay is dedicated—that a methodological pluralism is more fruitful. Thus, on one occasion I found meaning in the assumption of historico-critical scholars that the Peniel narrative originally told about a nocturnal encounter with a river spirit. This came to my mind when I visited a former student in his rather isolated rural parish. He told me that he could only visit the coolie families after sunset when they had returned from work in the fields, so that he often had to go long, lonely distances in the night. Once, parish members had anxiously warned him to avoid a particular desolate road because of frightening water spirits dwelling there. He went, all the same, after having told them that a Christian does not need to fear such spirits. However, it is an important question, how to relate to such deeply rooted and widespread beliefs regarding spirits. Is it only superstition, which can be fought with rational arguments or with the confidence of a superior Christian faith? Or is there a way to include traditional fears and taboos—as in the Jacob–Esau narrative—in the encounter and struggle with God over his blessing? The Christian encounter with traditional cultures and with people living in close contact with nature, its

rhythms, its blessings and threats, has often been purely destructive. Can it be that we can receive God's blessing only if we
encounter him or her as advocate, not only of the brother who
has been cheated, but also of nature which has not been
respected?

This question came back to my mind when I visited a remote
hill area inhabited by a small group of indigenous people. Development programmes had brought roads and electricity to the
area. On the newly constructed roads, lorries were carrying away
the wealth of the forest. In no time, devastating deforestation had
left the hills barren. Only one hill had escaped. The reason? On
its top resided an awe-inspiring deity who did not allow people to
cut any tree or even to enter the forest. People would go up only
on certain festival days, with offerings. Friendly visitors were pro-
hibited even if they were clearly not carrying axes or saws. I don't
know how long this helpful taboo will last, but it seems clear that
many 'enlightened' Christians have reason to stop and think why
their understanding of mastery over nature has not included a
sense of protection.

In May 1987 I was invited to Sri Lanka to do a series of Bible
studies on church and state. The armed conflict with separatist
Tamil groups had just reached a new stage of escalation. Tamil
'Tigers' had attacked buses and killed random Sinhala travellers.
The government had started a military offensive in the North and
bombarded Jaffna from the air. Both sides claimed to be fighting
for 'liberation'. The dominant guerrilla movement of the Tamils
calls itself 'Liberation Tigers for Tamil Eelam', and the military
offensive was conducted under the name 'Operation Liberation'.
Apart from that the extremist Sinhala underground movement
called the 'People's Liberation Movement' (JVP) was running a
bombing campaign in the South.

In past years I had noticed, to my distress, that several Tamil
students from Sri Lanka tended to identify the biblical vision of
liberation with the struggle and program of the LTTE, without
further qualification. Certainly, the Tamils have serious reasons to
fight against the violation of their rights. But many important
considerations speak against separatism as a sustainable and liberating solution. Even if successful, it would have to be a military
state permanently on its guard, probably largely dependent on

India and repressive towards its new minorities. In this context the Jacob–Esau story gave me a different biblical perspective on the conflict. Andre Dumas's reflections on 'fratriarchal relationships' (1978) and an exegesis of Gerard Minnaard (1987) helped me in this. Exodus from slavery, uprising against despotic rule, is not the only model of political conflicts. This is easily forgotten in an ideological climate which has been shaped by anti-imperialist, national liberation struggles. There are bloody conflicts in which the goal of the struggle for freedom from oppression and exploitation is not exodus or expulsion but equal rights and redistribution of a shared heritage. The Bible tells not only of the Exodus from Egypt, but also of the struggle between brothers, Isaac and Ishmael, Jacob and Esau, which may be as bitter, but which is meant to result in reconciliation.

It makes more biblical and political sense to understand the ethnic conflict in Sri Lanka as such a struggle between brothers. The central issue is, then, the sharing of the blessing.

The narratives about the patriarchs which precede the Exodus story have a political dimension. They reflect also on the history of the relationship between Israel and its neighbours, a history full of conflicts. The Jacob–Esau story, Genesis 25–35, narrates in a paradigmatic way how two sons, two neighbour peoples, Israel and Edom, fought over the one blessing. King David succeeded in subjugating Edom and in forcing it to pay tribute (2 Sam. 8.14). Afterwards there followed a long history of rule, uprising and warfare. Both tried to employ the 'help' of the imperial big powers against each other (see, e.g., 2 Chron. 28.16-17). Edom exploits the opportunity of Israel's defeat in the year 587 BCE to occupy— with Babylonian permission—the southern part of Judah. Some of the most violent and aggressive texts of the First Testament arise from this bitter experience with neighbouring Edom. The whole book of the prophet Obadiah speaks of that 'violence done to your brother Jacob' (v. 10). It was 'because you cherished perpetual enmity', says Ezekiel, that you 'gave over the people of Israel to the power of the sword at the time of their calamity' (Ezek. 35.5), and he announces that 'blood will pursue you' (v. 6). Human history is full of such endless chain reactions of shedding blood, repression, uprising, revenge and dreams of revenge, until today.

The Bible invites us to understand such bloody conflicts as
battles between brothers, as struggles over claims and rights, over
the proper share in God's blessing. That opens a perspective of
hope. Brothers can kill each other—as we know from the Cain–
Abel story. But they are meant to be reconciled with each other,
as Jacob and Esau were. Peace is possible, as their father, Isaac,
demonstrates at the outset of the Jacob–Esau story when he makes
a covenant with the Philistine King Abimelech after a conflict
about water resources (Gen. 26). Think of Israelis and Palestini-
ans today—peace becomes possible if the parties concerned are
able to reflect self-critically about the past. That is what Israel does
in exile. The Genesis stories about the 'patriarchs' reflect in their
present form such a critical retrospect. The experience of having
been deprived of God's blessing, having lost the land, brings the
self-critical insight that one has tried to deprive others of their
share. That is the promising alternative to the uncritical
glorification of one's own history, which is one of the most solid
obstacles on the way to peace between hostile peoples.

The biblical story remains realistic. It does not romanticize
about fraternity: already in the womb the two are quarrelling and
the hostility seems to be insurmountable (Gen. 25.22). In patriarchal society only one can become the bearer of the blessing. The
younger one is chosen. That excludes self-glorification. He has no
claims on the basis of birthright to one or the other form of superiority. Yet, the oracle in Gen. 25.23-24 could, for example, in the
time of David, be interpreted in such a way that it could serve as
an ideological legitimation of conquest and subjugation. Or, was
there an alternative possibility of service between brothers, in a
peaceful way, without domination? That is the question which is
thrown up in the course of the further story. First we hear—after
the concluding of the covenant of peace between Isaac and
Abimelech—how Esau is being cheated and loses the blessing.
'When Esau heard the words of his father, he cried out with an
exceedingly great and bitter cry, and said to his father, "Bless me,
even me also, O my father"' (Gen. 27.34). It is impressive to hear
with how much concern and empathy the narrator—who is from
the people of Israel!—presents the suffering of the brother who
has been cheated, when we remember the violent texts directed
against Edom quoted above. Such empathy, the capacity to see a

particular history through the eyes of the other, is a further condition for the birth of new relationships.

Esau asks for a separate blessing (v. 36). That would be the ideal solution of so many bitter conflicts. But the answer is 'No'. There is only one blessing, and Jacob has now become its bearer, whereas 'all his brothers' will be for him as 'servants'. Does that mean that the brothers—sisters are not mentioned in this patriarchal text—are going away empty-handed? Does blessing mean for the chosen one that he can live at the cost of the others? In the blessing passed on by Isaac to Jacob it is said: 'May God give you of the dew of heaven and of the fatness of the earth' (27. 28), and that is the only blessing. In the 'blessing' for Esau the same expression reappears, but preceded by the Hebrew word *min* (from). The RSV translates, 'away from the fatness of the earth shall your dwelling be and away from the dew of heaven' (v. 39). That speaks of exclusion, and reflects the desert-like environment of Edom. But it sounds to me that the sympathetic narrator, by repeating the same expression modified in this way, intends to pose the question to his listeners: was it right that we have excluded Esau/Edom so much, though there was no other blessing left? Did we leave Edom any other choice but to take up the sword against us, which led to the bloody history of war, oppression and uprising? As the saying continues: 'By your sword you shall live, and you shall serve your brother; but when you break loose you shall break his yoke from your neck' (v. 40). The whole story which follows seems to be a call to learn from this bitter history: Jacob had to flee, to Aram, as later Israel had to go into exile. There he who had cheated was cheated himself by Laban. Further stories of envy and conflict, between Leah, Rachel and their sons follow. All this teaches us, suggests the narrator, that after our return from exile we have to make a new beginning. We have to accept God's critique, as Jacob did, and come around to the insight that the one blessing is inclusive, which means that we have to share as brothers. That brings us again to the story of Genesis 32–33.

Finally, sharing becomes possible when both understand what is enough. Esau says, 'I have enough, my brother; keep what you have for yourself' (33.9). Jacob insists on sharing, because he received the blessing as gift and because there is 'enough'

(33.11). This could be the starting point for a further reflection in today's context where so many bitter social conflicts are directly or indirectly caused by the organizing principle of the present global economy and its politics, namely, the principle of accumulation, which is dramatically opposed to saying 'it is enough, let me share'.

BIBLIOGRAPHY

Dumas, André
    1978   *Political Theology and the Life of the Church* (London: SCM Press).
Minnaard, Gerard
    1987   'Der Maechtigere wird dem Geringeren dienen', in *Texte und Kontexte* 10 33: 4-24.
Waskow, Arthur
    1978   *Godwrestling* (New York: Schocken Books).
Wielenga, Bas
    1998   *It's a Long Road to Freedom* (Madurai).

INDEXES

INDEX OF REFERENCES

OLD TESTAMENT

NEW TESTAMENT

OTHER SOURCES

INDEX OF AUTHORS